FIRST 50 SONGS

YOU SHOULD PLAY ON BARITONE UKULELE

T0195143

ISBN 978-1-5400-1208-1

7777 W. BLUEMOUND RD. P.O. BOX 13819 MILWAUKEE, WI 53213

Visit Hal Leonard Online at
www.halleonard.com

CONTENTS

Amazing Grace

Words by John Newton
From A Collection of Sacred Ballads
Traditional American Melody
From Carrell and Clayton's Virginia Harmony
Arranged by Edwin O. Excell

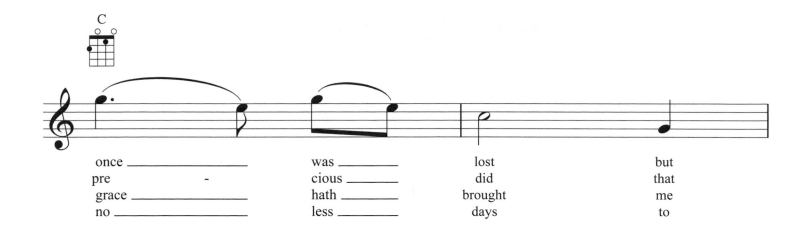

once	was	lost	but
pre -	cious	did	that
grace	hath	brought	me
no	less	days	to

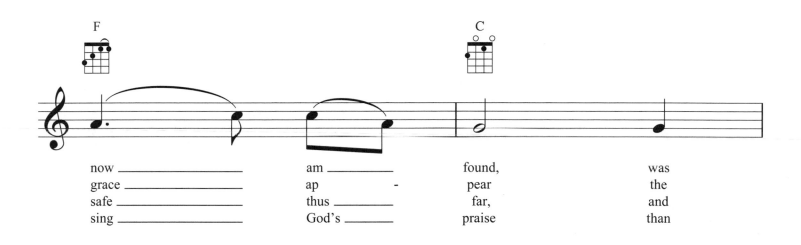

F   C

now	am	found,	was
grace	ap -	pear	the
safe	thus	far,	and
sing	God's	praise	than

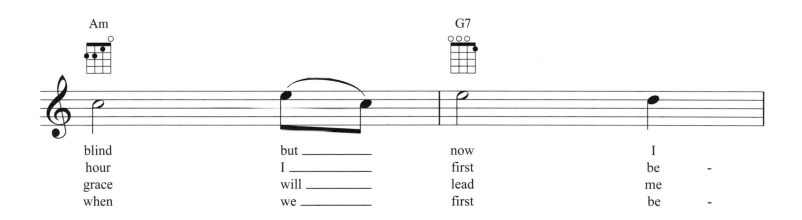

Am   G7

blind	but	now	I
hour	I	first	be -
grace	will	lead	me
when	we	first	be -

1.–3.   4.

C   C

see.	2. 'Twas	gun.
lieved.	3. Through	
home.	4. When	

Auld Lang Syne

Words by Robert Burns
Traditional Scottish Melody

Afternoon Delight

Words and Music by Bill Danoff

Verse

2., 4. Think-ing of you's work-ing up my ap - pe - tite, look-ing for-ward to a lit-tle af - ter-
(3.) out __ this __ morn-ing feel-ing so po - lite. I al-ways thought a fish could not be caught who

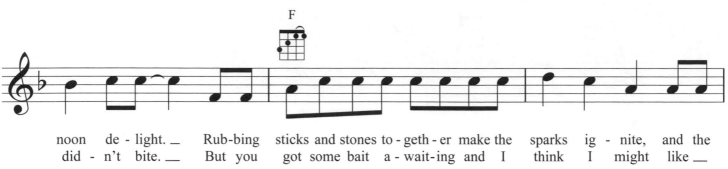

noon de - light. __ Rub-bing sticks and stones to - geth - er make the sparks ig - nite, and the
did - n't bite. __ But you got some bait a - wait-ing and I think I might like __

Chorus

thought of rub-bing you is get-ting so ex - cit - ing. } Sky rock-ets in flight,
nib - bl-ing a lit-tle af - ter - noon de - light. __ }

af - ter - noon __ de - light, af -

- ter - noon __ de - light, af -

To Coda ⊕

- ter - noon __ de - light. _____ 3. Start - ed

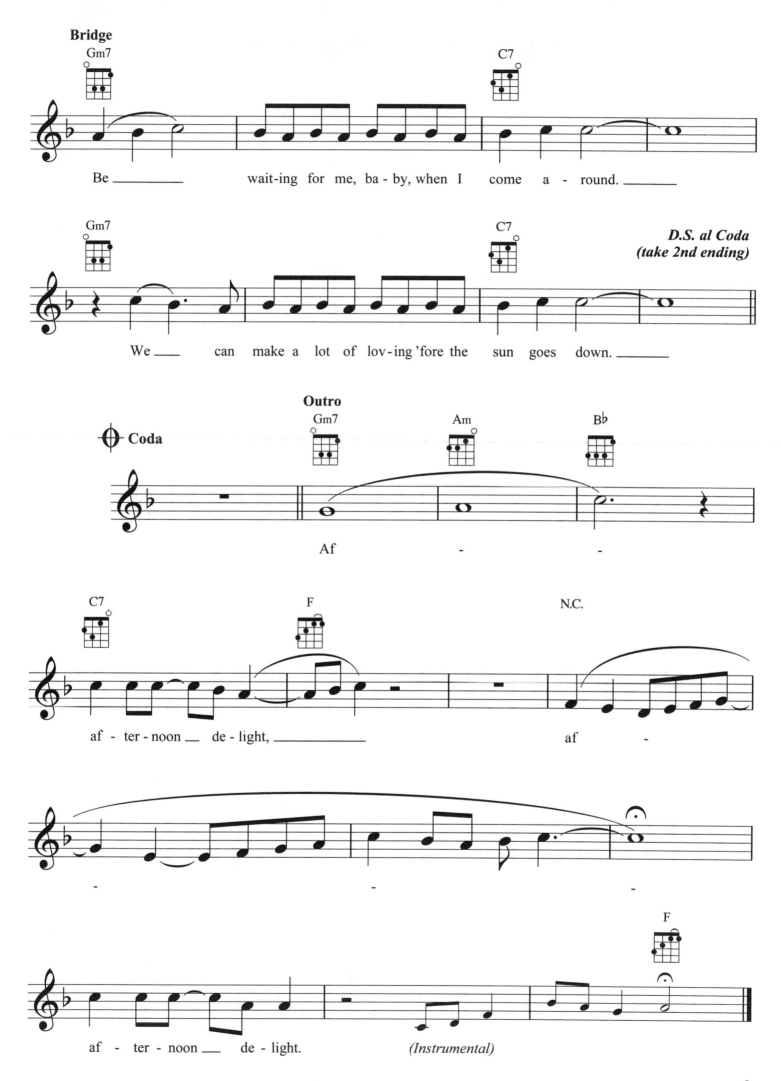

Bridge

Gm7   C7

Be _____ wait-ing for me, ba - by, when I come a - round. _____

Gm7   C7   ***D.S. al Coda*** *(take 2nd ending)*

We _____ can make a lot of lov-ing 'fore the sun goes down. _____

Outro

⊕ **Coda**   Gm7   Am   B♭

Af - -

C7   F   N.C.

af - ter - noon __ de - light, _____ af -

- - -

F

af - ter - noon __ de - light.   *(Instrumental)*

9

Blowin' in the Wind

Words and Music by Bob Dylan

non - balls ___ fly ___ be - fore ___ they are for -

- ev - er banned? ___ The an -

Chorus

- swer, my friend, ___ is blow - in' in ___ the wind. _

___ The an - swer is blow - in' in ___ the wind. _

1., 2.   3.

Additional Lyrics

2. How many years can a mountain exist
    Before it is washed to the sea?
    How many years can some people exist
    Before they're allowed to be free?
    Yes, and how many times can a man turn his head
    And pretend that he just doesn't see?

3. How many times must a man look up
    Before he can see the sky?
    How many ears must one man have
    Before he can hear people cry?
    Yes, and how many deaths will it take till he knows
    That too many people have died?

Both Sides Now

Words and Music by Joni Mitchell

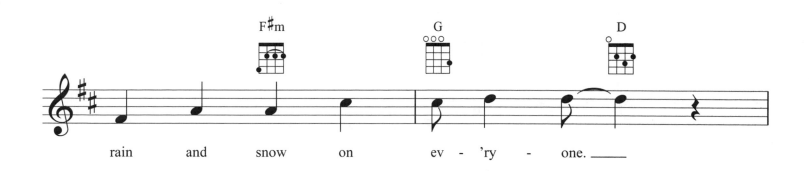

rain and snow on ev - 'ry - one. ____

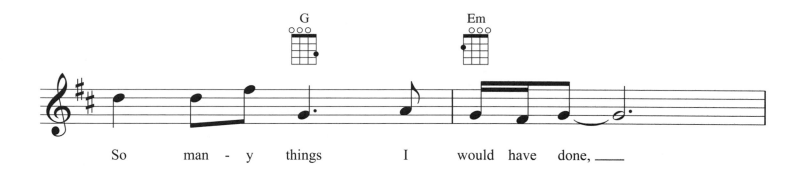

So man - y things I would have done, ____

but clouds ____ got in my ____ way. I've

Chorus

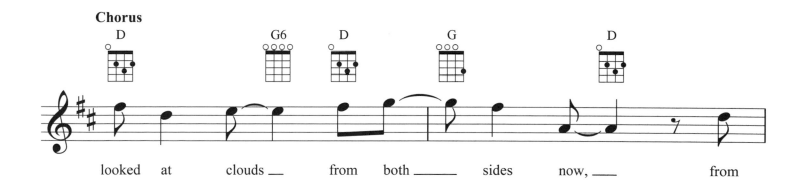

looked at clouds ____ from both ____ sides now, ____ from

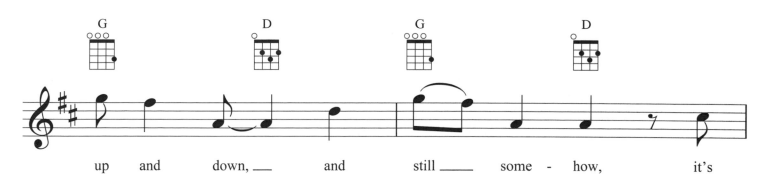

up and down, ____ and still ____ some - how, it's

Additional Lyrics

2. Moons and Junes and Ferris wheels,
   The dizzy dancing way you feel
   When ev'ry fairy tale comes real;
   I've looked at love that way.
   But now it's just another show.
   You leave 'em laughing when you go.
   And if you care, don't let them know,
   Don't give yourself away.

Chorus: I've looked at love from both sides now,
   From win and lose, and still somehow,
   It's love's illusions I recall.
   I really don't know love at all.

3. Tears and fears and feeling proud
   To say, "I love you" right out loud,
   Dreams and schemes and circus crowds;
   I've looked at life that way.
   But now old friends are acting strange.
   They shake their heads, they say I've changed.
   Well, something's lost and something's gained
   In living ev'ry day.

Chorus: I've looked at life from both sides now,
   From win and lose, and still somehow,
   It's life's illusions I recall.
   I really don't know life at all.

Boulevard of Broken Dreams

Words by Billie Joe
Music by Green Day

1. I walk a lone-ly road, the on-ly one that I _____ have ev-er known. _
2. I'm walk-ing down the line that di-vides me _ some-where in my

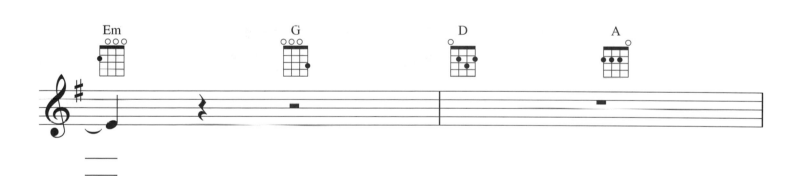

_____ Don't know where it goes, but it's home to me _____ and I walk a-lone.
mind, on the bor-der-line of the edge and _ where I walk a-lone. _

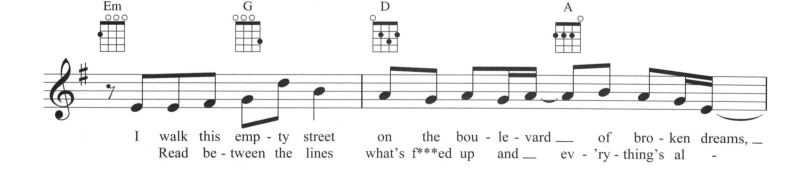

I walk this emp-ty street on the bou-le-vard _ of bro-ken dreams,
Read be-tween the lines what's f***ed up and _ ev-'ry-thing's al -

where the cit - y sleeps, and I'm the on - ly one __ } and I walk a - lone. __
right. Check my vi - tal signs and know I'm still a - live __

__ I walk a - lone, __ I walk a - lone. __

__ I walk a - lone, __ I walk a...

Chorus

My shad - ow's the on - ly one that walks __ be - side me.

My shal - low heart's __ the on - ly thing __ that's beat - ing.

Some - times __ I wish __ some - one out there __ will find me.

(Sittin' On) The Dock of the Bay

Words and Music by Steve Cropper and Otis Redding

Oo, ___ I'm just   sit - tin' on the dock of the bay, ___   wast - in' time. ___

2. I ___

Bridge

Look like   noth-in's gon - na   change; ___   ev - 'ry-thing

still re-mains the same.   I can't do what   ten peo-ple tell me ___ to do, ___

so   I guess I'll re - main ___ the same. ___   ___   (Whistling)

Outro

Repeat and fade

Edelweiss

from THE SOUND OF MUSIC
Lyrics by Oscar Hammerstein II
Music by Richard Rodgers

Bridge

Blos - som of snow, may you bloom and

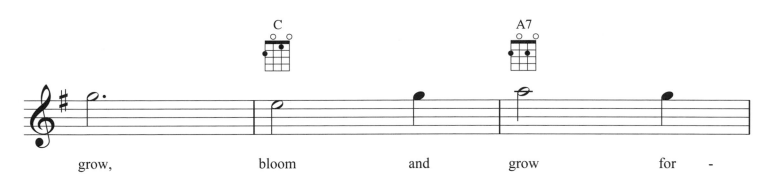

grow, bloom and grow for -

Chorus

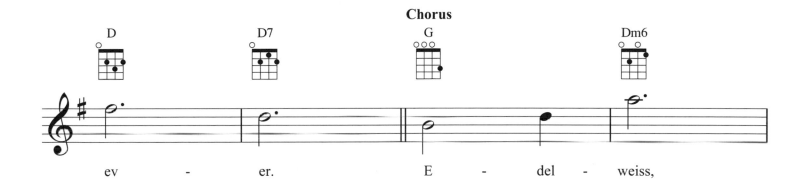

ev - er. E - del - weiss,

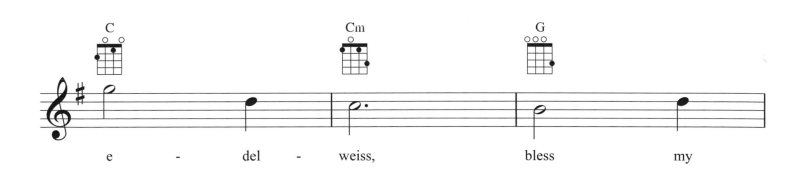

e - del - weiss, bless my

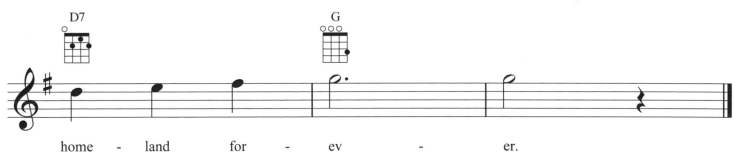

home - land for - ev - er.

Everything Is Beautiful

Words and Music by Ray Stevens

sum - mer night   or a   snow - cov - ered   win -   ter's

day.   Ev - 'ry - bod - y's   beau - ti - ful _____   in their own

way. _____   Un - der   God's   heav -   en,   the

To Coda

world's   gon - na   find _____   a   way. _____

Verse

1. There   is   none   so   blind ___   as   he   who   will   not
2. *See additional lyrics*

see. _____   We   must   not   close   our   minds, _____   we   must

23

Additional Lyrics

2. We shouldn't care about the length of his hair or the color of his skin.
Don't worry about what shows from without but the love that lies within.
We gonna get it all together now and everything's gonna work out fine.
Just take a little time to look on the good side, my friend, and straighten it out in your mind.

Escape

(The Piña Colada Song)

Words and Music by Rupert Holmes

there was this let-ter I read: ___   "If you like pi - ña co-

Chorus

la - das   and get - ting caught in the rain,

if you're not in - to yo - ga,   if you have half a

brain,   if you'd like mak - ing love at

mid - night ___   in the dunes on the Cape,

then I'm the love that you've looked for.

Write to me and es - cape."

(Instrumental)

Interlude

1., 2.

3.

2. I did - n't think a - bout my
3. So I wait - ed with ___

Additional Lyrics

2. I didn't think about my lady; I know that sounds kinda mean.
   But me and my old lady have fallen into the same old dull routine.
   So I wrote to the paper, took out a personal ad.
   And though I'm nobody's poet, I thought it wasn't half bad:
   "Yes, I like piña coladas and getting caught in the rain.
   I'm not much into health food; I am into champagne.
   I've got to meet you by tomorrow noon and cut through all this red tape,
   At a bar called O'Malley's, where we'll plan our escape."

3. So I waited with high hopes, and she walked in the place.
   I knew her smile in an instant, I knew the curve of her face.
   It was my own lovely lady, and she said, "Oh, it's you!"
   Then we laughed for a moment, and I said, "I never knew
   That you like piña coladas and getting caught in the rain,
   And the feel of the ocean and the taste of champagne.
   If you'd like making love at midnight in the dunes on the Cape,
   You're the lady I've looked for. Come with me and escape."

Gentle on My Mind

Words and Music by John Hartford

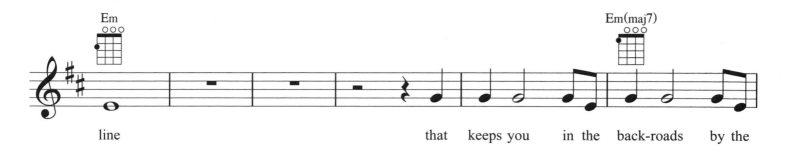

line   that keeps you in the back-roads by the

riv-ers of my mem-'ry that keeps you ev-er gen-tle on my

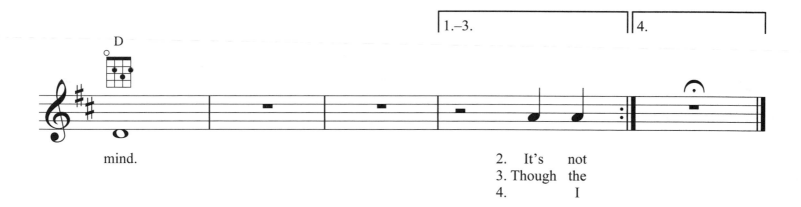

mind.

2. It's not
3. Though the
4.   I

Additional Lyrics

2. It's not clinging to the rocks and ivy planted on their columns now that bind me,
   Or something that somebody said because they thought we fit together walkin'.
   It's just knowing that the world will not be cursing or forgiving when I walk along some railroad track and find
   That you're moving on the backroad by the rivers of my memory, and for hours you're just gentle on my mind.

3. Though the wheat fields and the clotheslines and the junkyards and the highways come between us,
   And some other woman's crying to her mother 'cause she turned and I was gone.
   I still might run in silence, tears of joy might stain my face and a summer sun might burn me 'til I'm blind,
   But not to where I cannot see you walkin' on the backroads by the rivers flowing gentle on my mind.

4. I dip my cup of soup back from a gurglin', cracklin' caldron in some train yard,
   My beard, a roughening coal pile and a dirty hat pulled low across my face.
   Through cupped hands 'round the tin can I pretend I hold you to my breast and find
   That you're waiting from the backroads by the rivers of my memories, ever smilin', ever gentle on my mind.

Hallelujah

Words and Music by Leonard Cohen

First note

Verse
Moderately slow, in 2

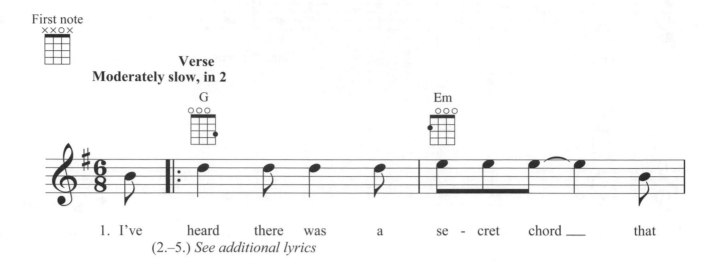

1. I've heard there was a se-cret chord ___ that
(2.–5.) *See additional lyrics*

Da-vid played ___ and it pleased the Lord, ___ but you don't ___ real-ly

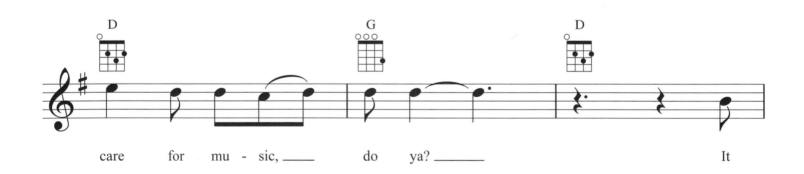

care for mu-sic, ___ do ya? ___ It

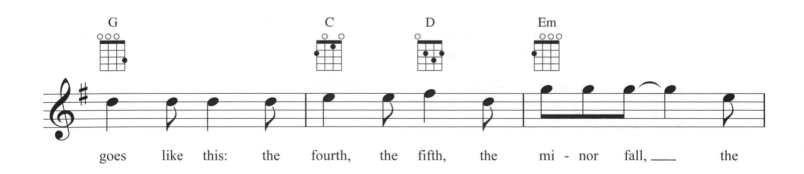

goes like this: the fourth, the fifth, the mi-nor fall, ___ the

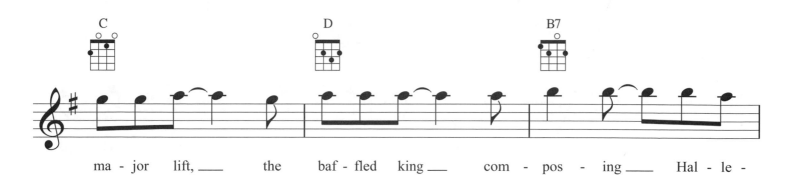

ma - jor lift, ___ the baf - fled king ___ com - pos - ing ___ Hal - le -

Chorus

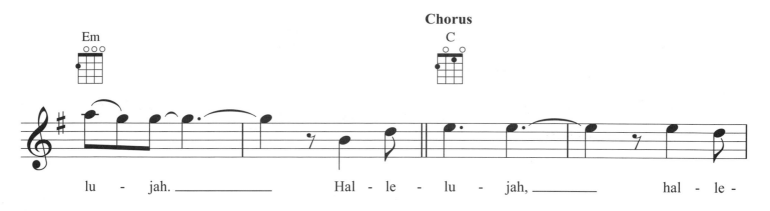

lu - jah. ___ Hal - le - lu - jah, ___ hal - le -

lu - jah, ___ hal - le - lu - jah, ___ hal - le -

1.–4.

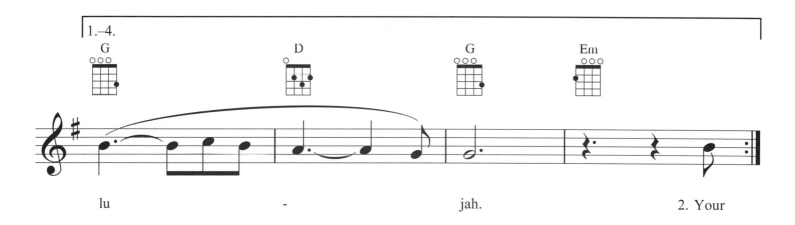

lu - jah. 2. Your

5.   **Outro-Chorus**

lu - jah. Hal - le - lu - jah. ___ Hal - le -

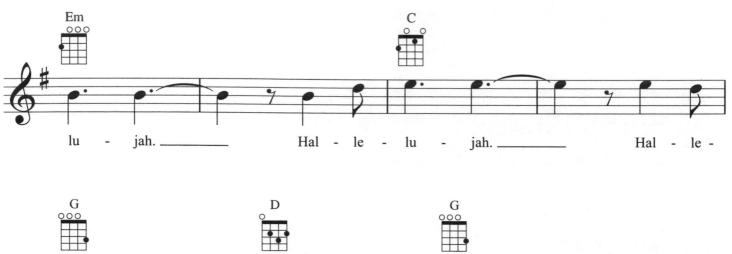

lu - jah. _____ Hal - le - lu - jah. _____ Hal - le -

lu - jah. _____

Additional Lyrics

2. Your faith was strong but you needed proof.
   You saw her bathing on the roof.
   Her beauty and the moonlight overthrew ya.
   She tied you to a kitchen chair.
   She broke your throne, she cut your hair.
   And from your lips she drew the Hallelujah.

3. Maybe I have been here before.
   I know this room, I've walked this floor.
   I used to live alone before I knew ya.
   I've seen your flag on the marble arch.
   Love is not a vict'ry march.
   It's a cold and it's a broken Hallelujah.

4. There was a time you let me know
   What's real and going on below.
   But now you never show it to me, do ya?
   And remember when I moved in you.
   The holy dark was movin', too,
   And every breath we drew was Hallelujah.

5. Maybe there's a God above,
   And all I ever learned from love
   Was how to shoot at someone who outdrew ya.
   And it's not a cry you can hear at night.
   It's not somebody who's seen the light.
   It's a cold and it's a broken Hallelujah.

The 59th Street Bridge Song
(Feelin' Groovy)
Words and Music by Paul Simon

First note

Verse
Happily, in 2

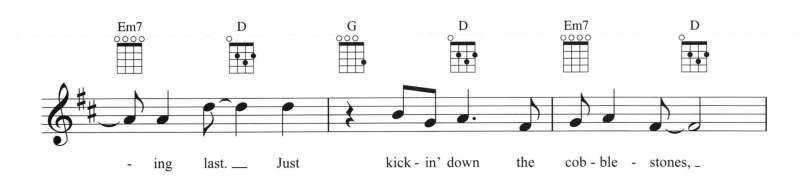

1. Slow down, __ you move too fast. __ You got to make the morn -

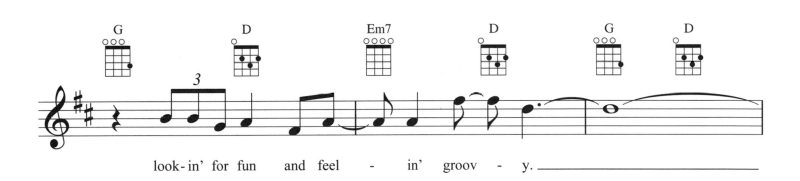

- ing last. __ Just kick - in' down the cob - ble - stones, __

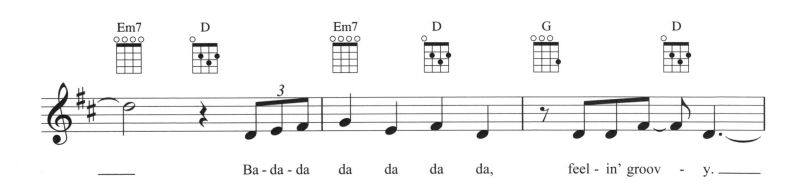

look - in' for fun and feel - in' groov - y. __

__ Ba - da - da da da da da, feel - in' groov - y. __

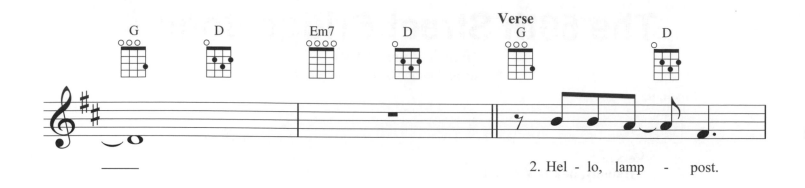

Verse

2. Hel - lo, lamp - post.

What - cha know - in'? I've come to watch your flow - ers grow - in'.

Ain't you got no rhymes _____ for me? Dwit - n - doo - doo,

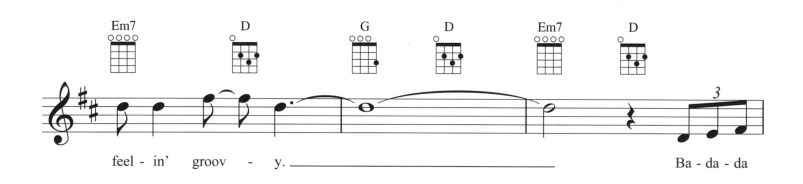

feel - in' groov - y. _____ Ba - da - da

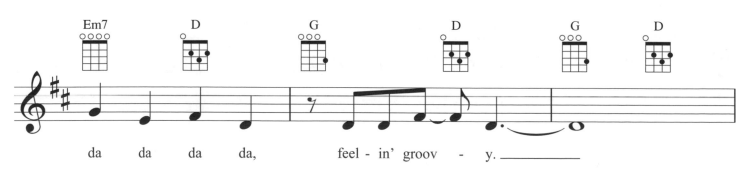

da da da da, feel - in' groov - y. _____

Verse

3. I got no deeds to do, no prom-is-es _____ to keep. I'm

dap-pled and drow-sy and read-y to sleep. Let the morn-ing-time drop all its

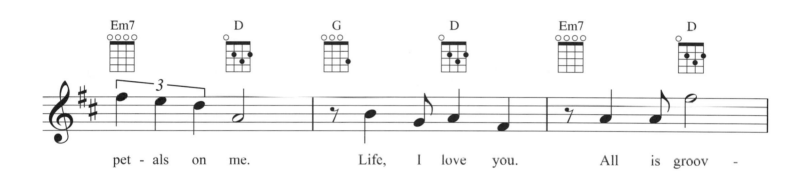

pet-als on me. Life, I love you. All is groov -

Outro

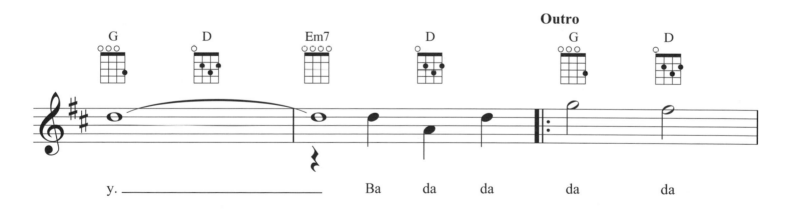

y. _____ Ba da da da da

Repeat and fade

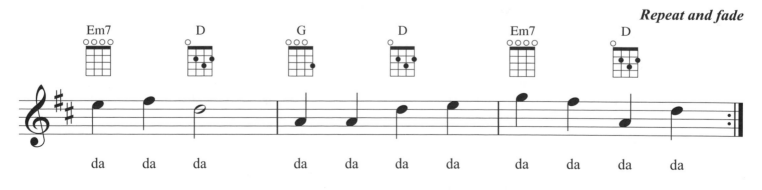

da da da da da da da da da da da

Happy Together

Words and Music by Gary Bonner and Alan Gordon

37

Hey, Soul Sister

Words and Music by Pat Monahan, Espen Lind and Amund Bjorklund

the smell of you __ in ev - 'ry sin - gle dream I __ dream. _

__ I knew when we col - lid - ed, you're the one __ I have de -

cid - ed who's one of my __ kind. __

𝄋 **Chorus**

Hey, soul __ sis - ter, ain't __ that Mis - ter Mis - ter on the

ra - di - o, __ ster - e - o? __ The way __ you move __ ain't fair, you know. __

To Coda ⊕

Hey, soul __ sis - ter, I __ don't wan - na miss a sin - gle

1.

Interlude

thing you do ___ to - night. ___ Hey, ___

___ hey, ___ hey. ___

2.

Bridge

___ to - night. ___ The way you can cut a rug, ___

watch-ing you's __ the on - ly drug __ I need. __ Some gang - sta, I'm __ so thug. _You're the

on - ly one __ I'm dream - in' of. ___ You see, I can be my - self now, fi - nal-ly.

In fact, __ there's noth in' I ___ can't be. ___ I want the world to see __ you'll

Additional Lyrics

2. Just in time, I'm so glad you have a one-track mind like me.
   You gave my life direction,
   A game-show love connection we can't deny.
   I'm so obsessed, my heart is bound to beat right out my untrimmed chest.
   I believe in you. Like a virgin, you're Madonna
   And I'm always gonna wanna blow your mind.

I Walk the Line

Words and Music by John R. Cash

First note

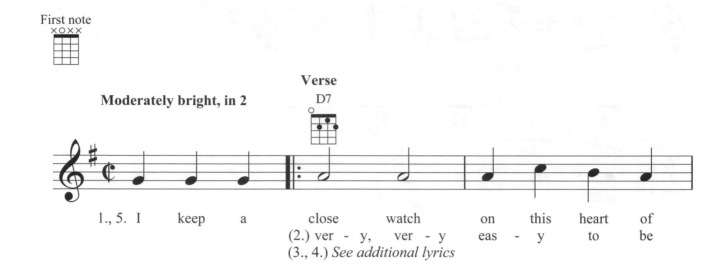

Moderately bright, in 2

Verse

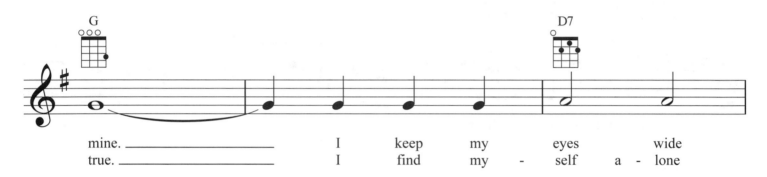

1., 5. I keep a close watch on this heart of
(2.) ver - y, ver - y eas - y to be
(3., 4.) *See additional lyrics*

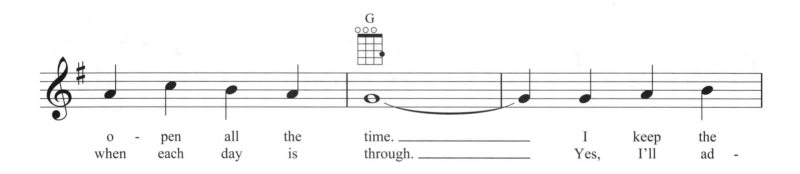

mine. _____ I keep my eyes wide
true. _____ I find my - self a - lone

o - pen all the time. _____ I keep the
when each day is through. _____ Yes, I'll ad -

ends out for the tie that binds. _____
mit that I'm a fool for you. _____

Be - cause you're mine, _____

1.–4.
G

_____ I walk the line. _____

5.
G

2. I find it line. _____
3. As sure as
4. You've got a

Additional Lyrics

    3. As sure as night is dark and day is light,
         I keep you on my mind both day and night.
         And happiness I've known proves that it's right.
         Because you're mine, I walk the line.

    4. You've got a way to keep me on your side.
         You give me a cause for love that I can't hide.
         For you I know I'd even try to turn the tide.
         Because you're mine, I walk the line.

I'd Like to Teach the World to Sing

Words and Music by Bill Backer, Roquel Davis, Roger Cook and Roger Greenaway

1. I'd like to build __ the world __ a home __ and
(2., 3.) See additional lyrics

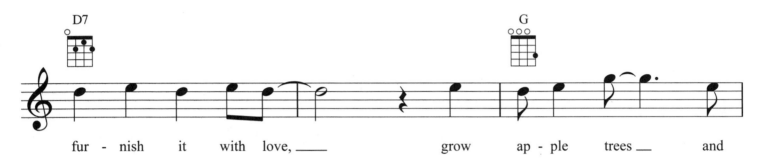

fur - nish it with love, ___ grow ap - ple trees __ and

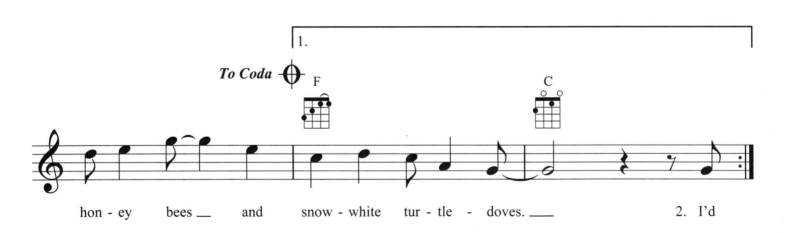

hon - ey bees __ and snow - white tur - tle - doves. ___ 2. I'd

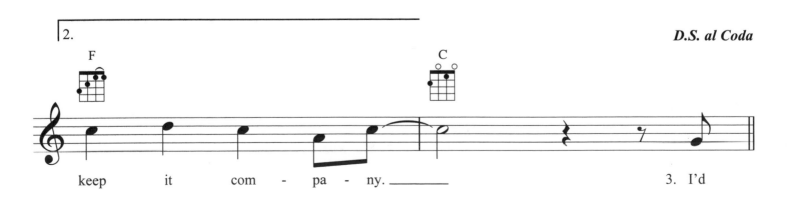

keep it com - pa - ny. ___ 3. I'd

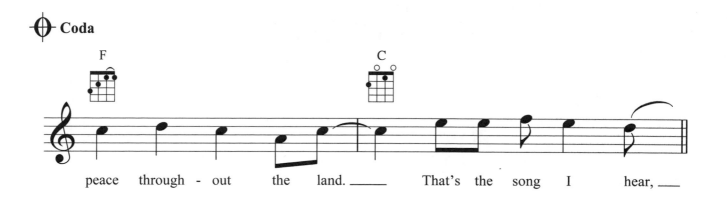

$\oplus$ **Coda**

peace through - out the land. ____ That's the song I hear, ___

Bridge

____ let the world sing to - day.

Outro

I'd like to teach ___ the world ___ to sing ___ in

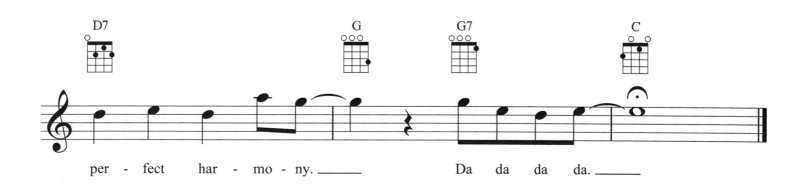

per - fect har - mo - ny. _____ Da da da da. _____

Additional Lyrics

2. I'd like to teach the world to sing in perfect harmony.
   I'd like to hold it in my arms and keep it company.

3. I'd like to see the world, for once, all standing hand in hand,
   And hear them echo through the hills for peace throughout the land.

I'm Yours

Words and Music by Jason Mraz

reck-on it's a-gain my turn _____ to win some ___ or learn some. } But
what we aim to do. Our name is ___ our vir - tue. } But

Chorus

I won't hes - i - tate no more, no more. It

To Coda ⊕

can - not wait. I'm yours. _____

Bridge

2. Well, o-pen up your mind and see ___ like me. ___ O - pen up your

plans and, damn, ___ you're free. ___ Look in - to your heart and you'll ___ find

love,   love, _____ love,   love.   Lis - ten to the mu - sic of the

mo - ment; peo - ple dance _ and sing.   We're just one big fam - i - ly, _

____ and it's our god - for - sak - en right to be loved,   loved, _____

loved,   loved,   loved. _____   So,

Chorus

I   won't   hes - i - tate   no   more,   no

more.   It   can - not   wait.   I'm   sure _____ there's no

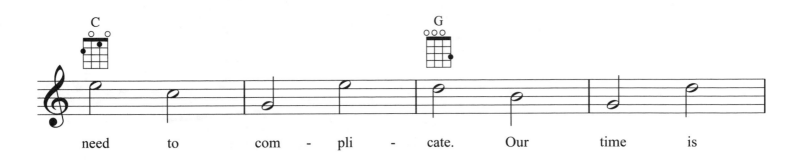

need   to   com - pli - cate.   Our   time   is

short.   This   is   our   fate.   I'm   yours. _____   *Scat...*

Interlude

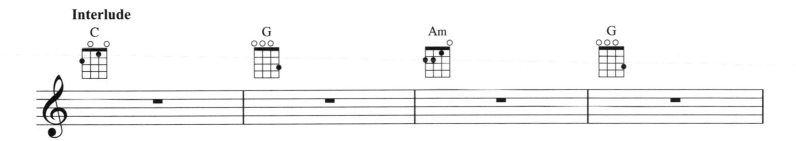

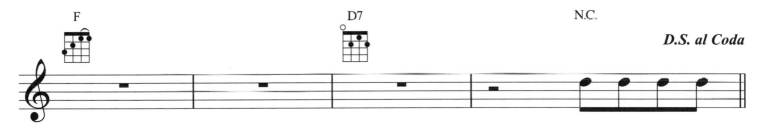

D.S. al Coda

3. I've been spend - ing

⊕ **Coda**   **Bridge/Chorus**

yours. _____   Well, o - pen up your   mind   and see   like
(I   won't   hes -   i -

me.   O - pen up your   plans and, damn, _ you're   free.   Look in - to your
tate   no   more,   no   more.   It

heart   and   you'll _   find   that   the   sky   is   yours. _____   So,
can   -   not   wait   I'm   sure. _____   No

please   don't,   please   don't,   please   don't...   There's   no   need __   to   com - pli -
need   to   com   -   pli   -   cate.   Our

cate   'cause   our   time   is   short. _   This   is,   this   is,   this   is   our
time   is   short.   This   is   our

fate.   I'm   yours. _____   Scat...
fate.   I'm   yours.) _____

Outro

Repeat and fade

Imagine

Words and Music by John Lennon

Chorus

___ you may say _____ I'm a dream-er, but I'm not the on-ly one. I hope some day _____ you'll join us _____ and the world _____ will

1. be as one. _____

2. live as one. _____

Additional Lyrics

3. Imagine no possessions,
   I wonder if you can;
   No need for greed or hunger,
   A brotherhood of man.
   Imagine all the people sharing all the world.

If I Had a Hammer
(The Hammer Song)

Words and Music by Lee Hays and Pete Seeger

love   be - tween   my   broth - ers   and   my   sis - ters,

all _____   o - ver   this

|1.–3.

land.   2., 3. If   I   had   a
        4. Well,   I   got   a

|4.

land. _____

Additional Lyrics

2. If I had a bell, I'd ring it in the morning,
   I'd ring it in the evening all over this land.
   I'd ring out danger, I'd ring out a warning,
   I'd ring out love between my brothers and my sisters,
   All over this land.

3. If I had a song, I'd sing it in the morning,
   I'd sing it in the evening all over this land.
   I'd sing out danger, I'd sing out a warning,
   I'd sing out love between my brothers and my sisters,
   All over this land.

4. Well, I got a hammer, and I've got a bell,
   And I've got a song to sing all over this land.
   It's the hammer of justice, it's the bell of freedom,
   It's the song about love between my brothers and my sisters,
   All over this land.

Jambalaya
(On the Bayou)

Words and Music by Hank Williams

Chorus

F

Jam - ba - la - ya, and a craw-fish pie, and fil - let

C7

gum - bo. _____ 'Cause to - night I'm gon - na

F

see my ma cher a mi - o. _____ Pick gui - tar, _____

C7

_____ fill fruit jar, and be gay - o. _____

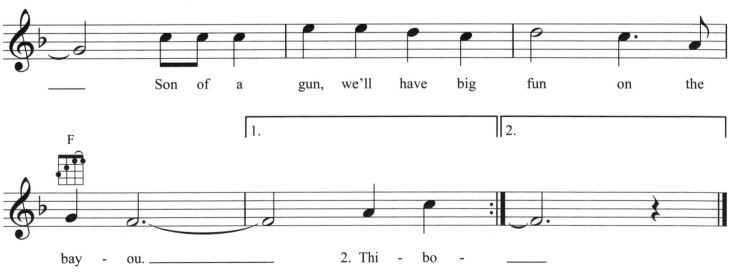

_____ Son of a gun, we'll have big fun on the

1.   2.

F

bay - ou. _____ 2. Thi - bo - _____

Love Me Tender

Words and Music by Elvis Presley and Vera Matson

Leaving on a Jet Plane

Words and Music by John Denver

blow - in' his horn. __ Al - read - y I'm so lone - some I could
sing for you. __ When I come back I'll bring your wed - ding
leave a - lone, __ a - bout the times I won't have to

Chorus

die. _____ So kiss
ring. _____ So kiss ⎫ me and smile for me, __
say: _____ Kiss ⎭

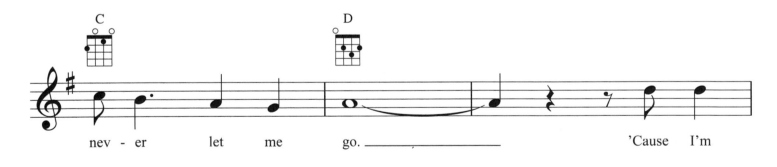

tell me that __ you'll wait for me, __ hold me like __ you'll

nev - er let me go. _____ 'Cause I'm

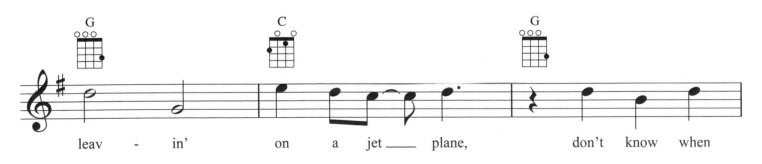

leav - in' on a jet __ plane, don't know when

I'll be back __ a-gain. _____ Oh, babe, I hate to

1., 2.

3.

go. _____ 2. There's so go. _____

Outro

___ I'm leav - in' on a jet __ plane, don't know when

I'll be back __ a-gain. _____ Oh, babe, _____ I hate to

go. _____

Mack the Knife

from THE THREEPENNY OPERA

English Words by Marc Blitzstein
Original German Words by Bert Brecht
Music by Kurt Weill

First note

Verse

Moderately, in 2

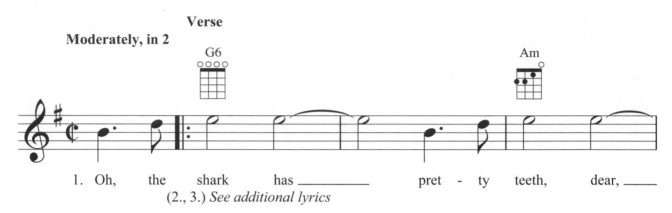

1. Oh,   the   shark   has _____ pret - ty   teeth,   dear, _____
(2., 3.) *See additional lyrics*

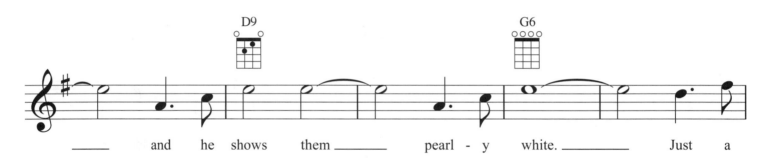

_____ and   he   shows   them _____ pearl - y   white. _____ Just   a

jack - knife _____ has   Mac - heath,   dear, _____ and   he   keeps   it

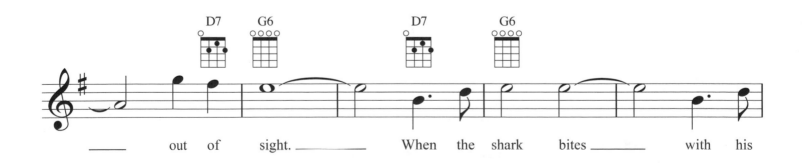

_____ out   of   sight. _____ When   the   shark   bites _____ with   his

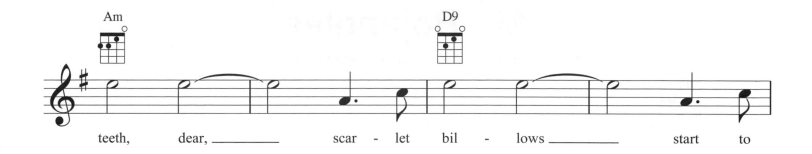

teeth, dear, _____ scar - let bil - lows _____ start to

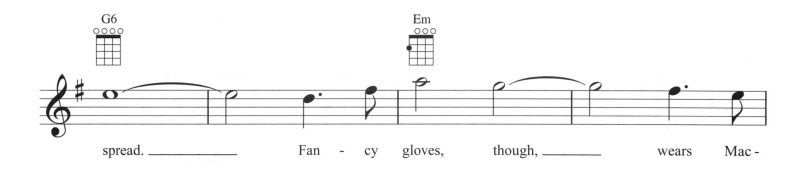

spread. _____ Fan - cy gloves, though, _____ wears Mac -

heath, dear, _____ so there's not a _____ trace of

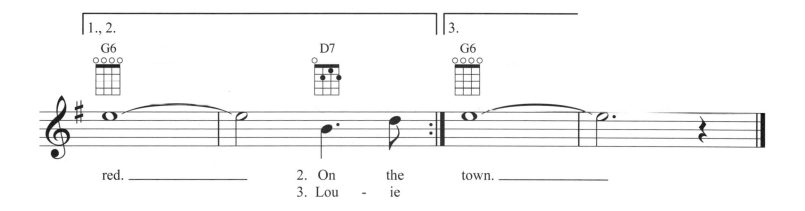

red. _____ 2. On the town. _____
3. Lou - ie

Additional Lyrics

2. On the sidewalk Sunday morning lies a body oozing life.
Someone's sneaking 'round the corner; is the someone Mack the Knife?
From a tugboat by the river, a cement bag's dropping down.
The cement's just for the weight, dear; bet you Mackie's back in town.

3. Louie Miller disappeared, dear, after drawing out his cash.
And Macheath spends like a sailor; did our boy do something rash?
Sukey Tawdry, Jenny Diver, Polly Peachum, Lucy Brown.
Oh, the line forms on the right, dear, now that Mackie's back in town.

Mr. Bojangles

Words and Music by Jerry Jeff Walker

First note

1. I knew a man, Bo - jan - gles, and he'd dance ___ for you
(2.–5.) *See additional lyrics*

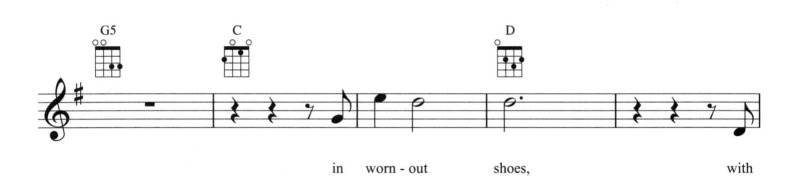

in worn - out shoes, with

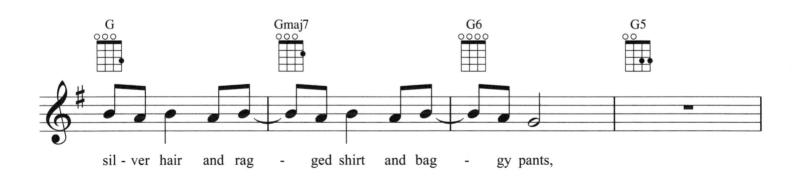

sil - ver hair and rag - ged shirt and bag - gy pants,

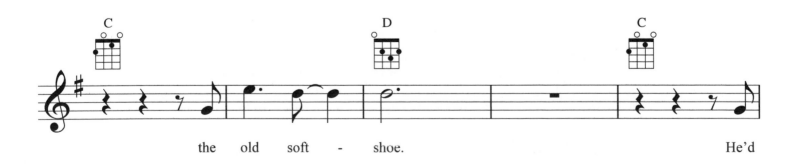

the old soft - shoe. He'd

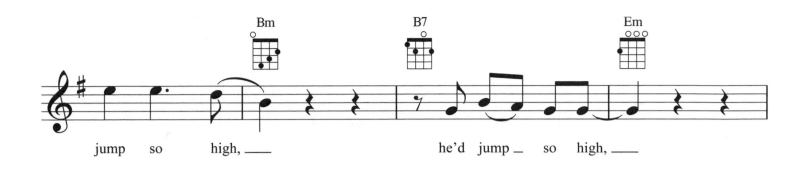

jump   so   high, ___   he'd   jump __   so   high, ___

and   then   he'd   light - ly   touch __   down. __

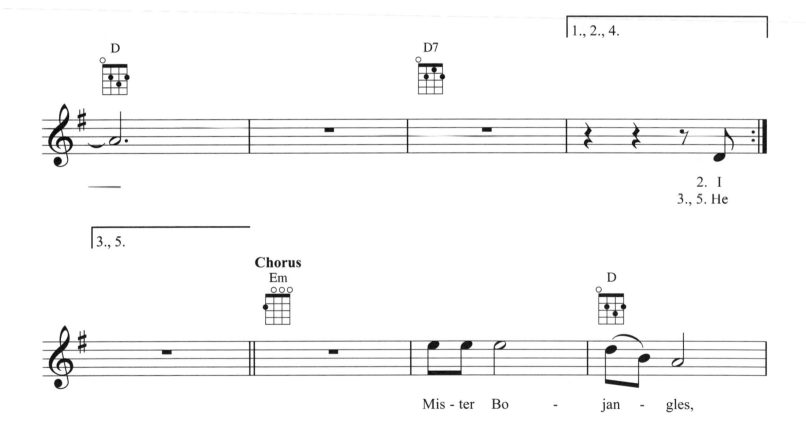

1., 2., 4.

___

2. I
3., 5. He

3., 5.

Chorus

Mis - ter   Bo -   jan -   gles,

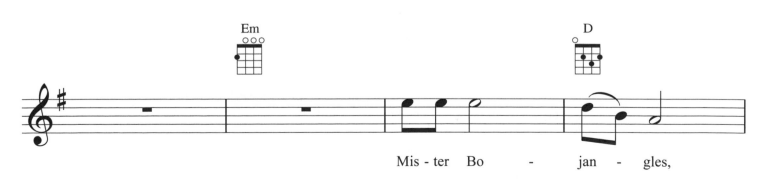

Mis - ter   Bo -   jan -   gles,

Mis - ter Bo - jan - gles,

To Coda ⊕

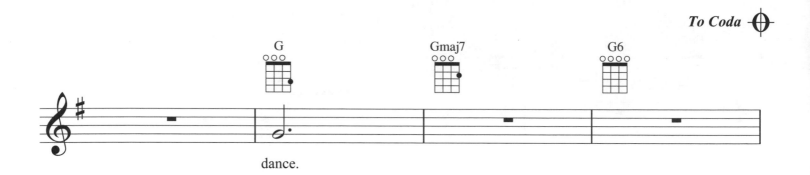

dance.

D.S. al Coda
(with repeat)

⊕ **Coda**

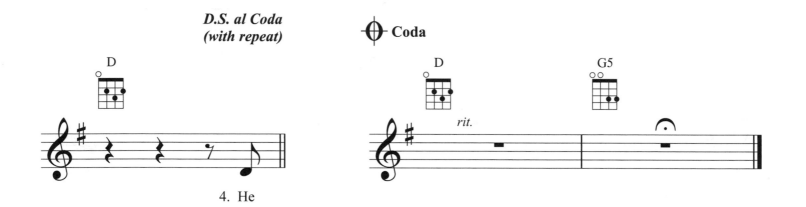

4. He

rit.

Additional Lyrics

2. I met him in a cell in New Orleans; I was down and out.
   He looked to me to be the eyes of age as the smoke ran out.
   He talked of life, he talked of life,
   Laughed, clicked his heels and stepped.

3. He said his name, Bojangles, and he danced a lick across the cell.
   He grabbed his pants in feathered stance 'fore he jumped so high,
   And then he clicked his heels.
   He let go a laugh, he let go a laugh,
   Shook back his clothes all around.

4. He danced for those at minstrel shows and county fairs throughout the South.
   He spoke with tears of fifteen years, how his dog and him traveled about.
   The dog up and died, he up and died.
   After twenty years, he still grieves.

5. He said, "I dance now at ev'ry chance in honky-tonks for drinks and tips.
   But most' the time I spend behind these county bars 'cause I drinks a bit."
   He shook his head, and as he shook his head,
   I heard someone ask him: Please, please...

Mr. Tambourine Man

Words and Music by Bob Dylan

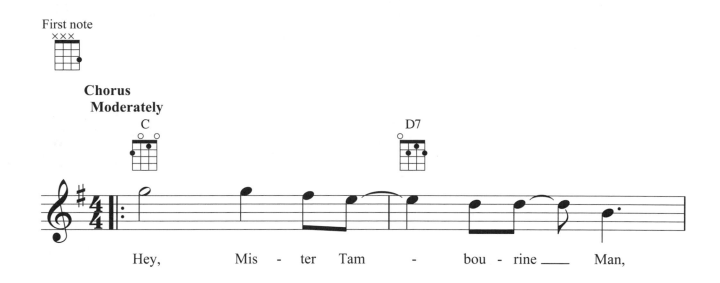

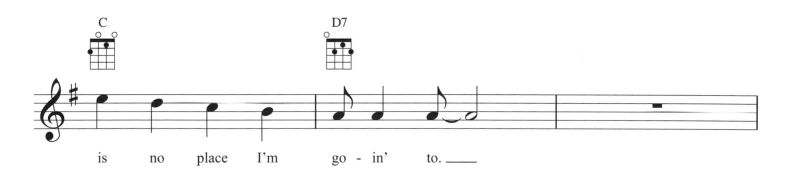

In the jin - gle jan - gle morn - in', I'll come

fol - low - in' you.

1. Though I
2.–4. *See additional lyrics*

Verse

know that eve - nin's em - pire _____ has re - turned in - to

sand, van - ished from __ my hand, left me

blind - ly here to stand, but still not sleep - ing.

My wea - ri - ness __ a - maz - es me, __ I'm

brand - ed on my feet, I have no one to

meet, and the an - cient emp - ty street's too dead for

1.–3. 4.

Coda

D.C. al Coda

dream - in'. _____ you.

Additional Lyrics

2. Take me on a trip upon your magic swirlin' ship.
   My senses have been stripped, my hands can't feel to grip.
   My toes too numb to step, wait only for my boot heels to be wanderin'.
   I'm ready to go anywhere, I'm ready for to fade
   Into my own parade, cast your dancin' spell my way.
   I promise to go under it.

3. Though you might hear laughin', spinnin', swingin' madly across the sun,
   It's not aimed at anyone, it's just escapin' on the run.
   And but for the sky, there are no fences facin',
   And if you hear vague traces of skippin' reels of rhyme
   To your tambourine in time, it's just a ragged clown behind.
   I wouldn't pay it any mind; it's just a shadow you're seein' that he's chasin'.

4. Then take me disappearin' through the smoke rings of my mind,
   Down the foggy ruins of time, far past the frozen leaves,
   The haunted, frightened trees out to the windy beach,
   Far from the twisted reach of crazy sorrow,
   Yes, to dance beneath the diamond sky with one hand wavin' free,
   Silhouetted by the sea, circled by the circus sands,
   With all memory and fate driven deep beneath the waves.
   Let me forget about today until tomorrow.

Monday, Monday

Words and Music by John Phillips

First note

Intro
Moderately

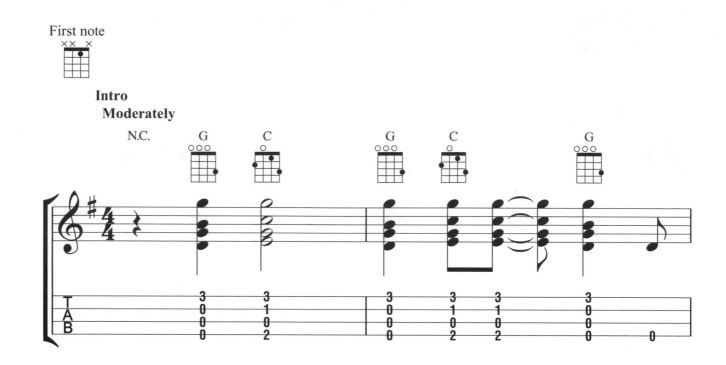

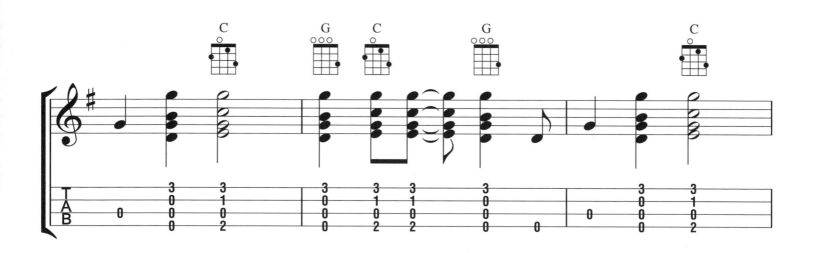

𝄋 Verse

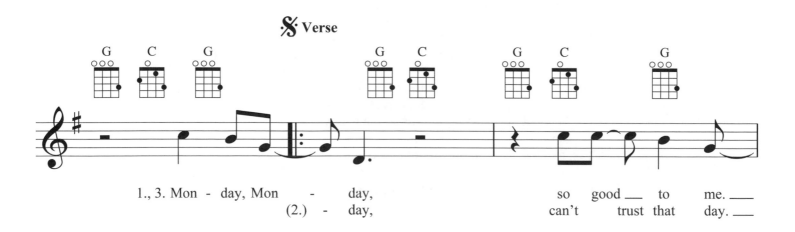

1., 3. Mon - day, Mon - day,   so good __ to me. __
     (2.) - day,   can't trust that day. __

Bridge

Ev-'ry oth-er day, ___ ev-'ry oth-er day, ev-'ry oth-er day of the week is

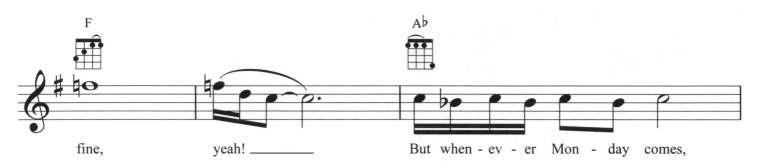

fine, yeah! _____ But when-ev-er Mon-day comes,

To Coda ⊕

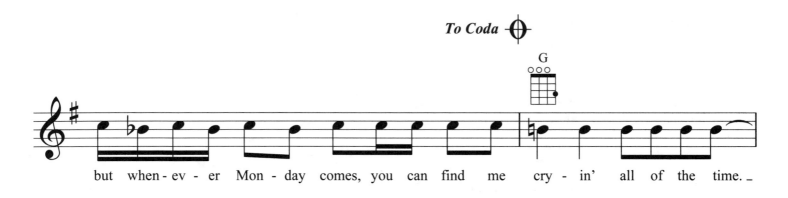

but when-ev-er Mon-day comes, you can find me cry-in' all of the time. ___

⊕ **Coda**

D.S. al Coda
(Lyric 1, take 2nd ending)

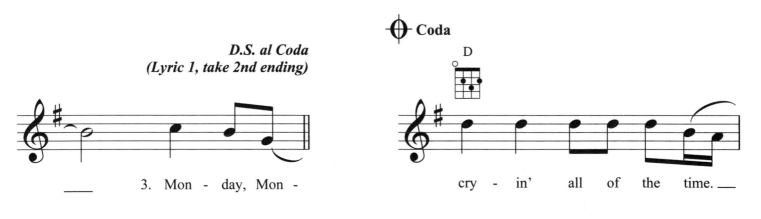

___ 3. Mon-day, Mon-   cry-in' all of the time. ___

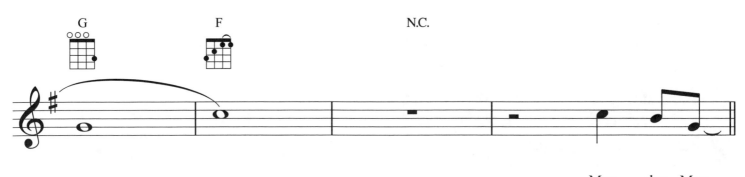

_____   Mon-day, Mon-

Outro-Verse

Over the Rainbow

from THE WIZARD OF OZ
Music by Harold Arlen
Lyric by E.Y. "Yip" Harburg

hind   me. _____   Where trou - bles melt like lem - on drops, a -

way, a - bove the chim - ney tops; that's where   you'll   find   me.

Verse

3. Some - where   o - ver the rain - bow,   blue - birds

fly.   Birds   fly   o - ver   the   rain - bow,

Outro

freely

why,   then, oh,   why   can't   I?   If   hap - py   lit - tle   blue-birds   fly   be -

yond   the   rain - bow,   why,   oh,   why   can't   I? _____

75

Peaceful Easy Feeling

Words and Music by Jack Tempchin

1. I like the way ___ your spar - klin' ear - rings ___
2., 3. *See additional lyrics*

lay a - gainst ___ your skin ___ so brown. ___

___ And I wan - na

sleep with you ___ in the des - ert ___ to - night, ___

with a bil - lion stars all a - round. ___

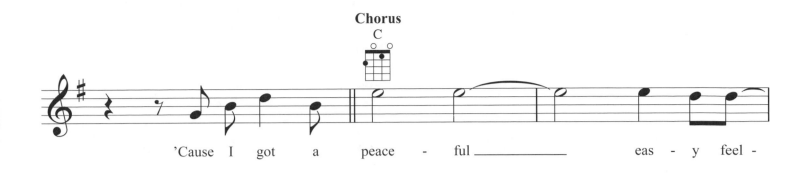

'Cause I got a peace - ful _____ eas - y feel -

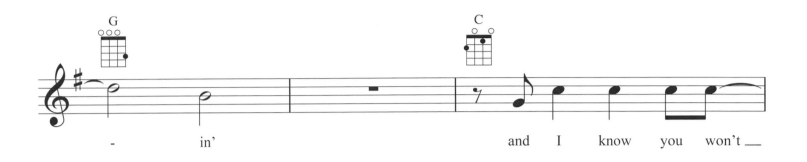

- in'   and I know you won't __

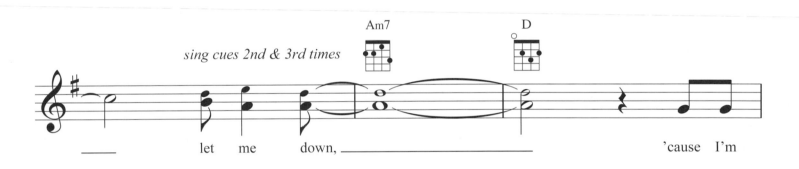

sing cues 2nd & 3rd times

___ let me down, _____ 'cause I'm

To Coda ⊕

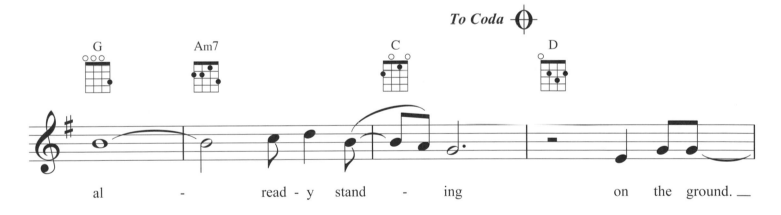

al - read - y stand - ing   on the ground. __

2nd time, D.C. al Coda

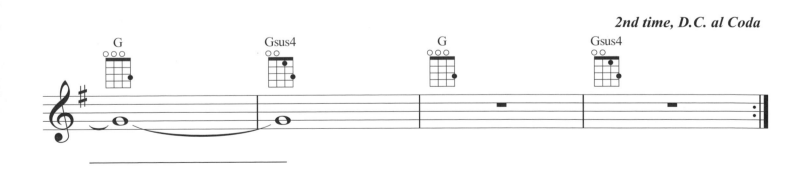

Additional Lyrics

2. And I found out a long time ago
   What a woman can do to your soul.
   Ah, but she can't take you any way
   You don't already know how to go.
   And I got a... *(To Chorus)*

3. I get this feeling I may know you
   As a lover and a friend.
   But this voice keeps whispering in my other ear;
   Tells me I may never see you again.
   'Cause I get a... *(To Chorus)*

One Toke Over the Line

Words and Music by Michael Brewer and Thomas E. Shipley

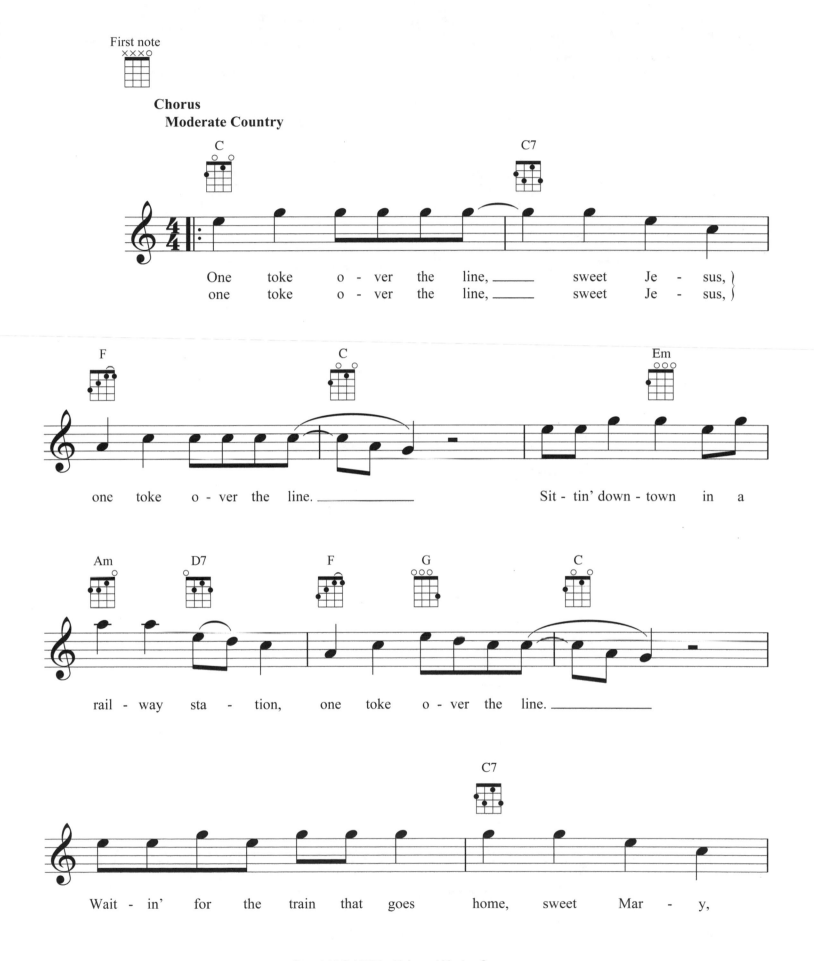

To Coda

Verse

1. Who _____ do you love? _____
2. I _____ sailed a - way _____

_____ I hope it's me. _____ I've been
_____ a coun - try mile, _____ and now I'm re -

chang - in', as you can plain - ly see. _____
turn - in' and show - in' off my smile. _____ I

I felt the joy and I learned a - bout the pain _____
met all the girls and I loved my - self a few, _____

___ that my ma - ma said. _____
___ when to my sur - prise, _____

If I should choose to make a part of me, _____
like ev - 'ry - thing else that I've been through, _____

2nd time, D.C. al Coda

would sure - ly strike me dead. ___ }
it o - pened up my eyes. ___ } And now I'm

Coda

Outro

C F D7 F G C

___ One ___ toke, one toke o - ver the line. ___

Pearly Shells
(Pupu O Ewa)

Words and Music by Webley Edwards and Leon Pober

First note

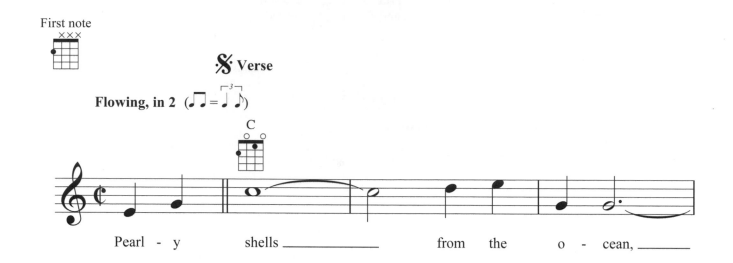

Pearl - y shells _____ from the o - cean, _____

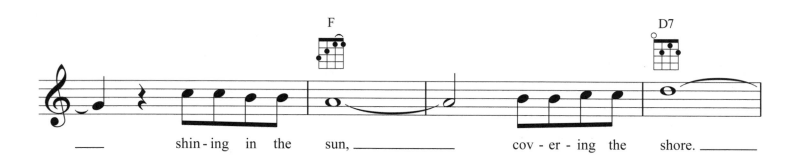

_____ shin - ing in the sun, _____ _____ cov - er - ing the shore. _____

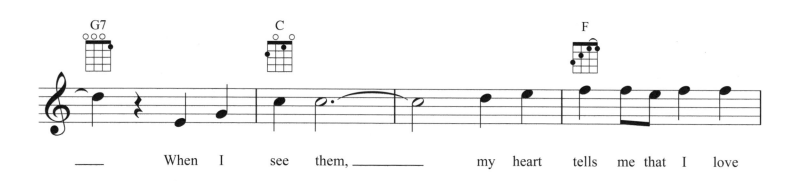

_____ When I see them, _____ my heart tells me that I love

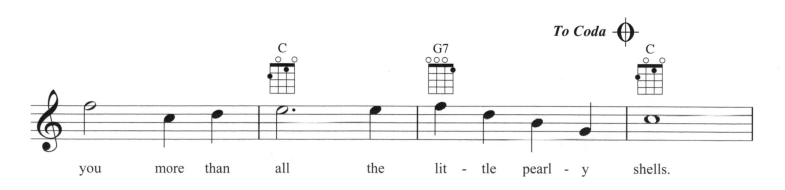

you more than all the lit - tle pearl - y shells.

Bridge

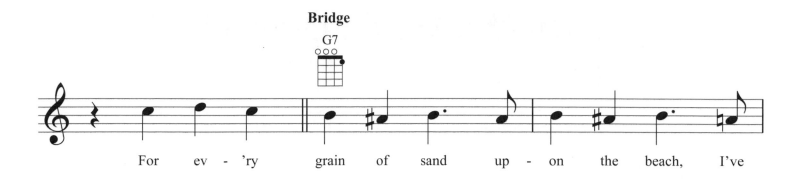

For ev - 'ry grain of sand up - on the beach, I've

got a kiss for you; and I've got more left o - ver

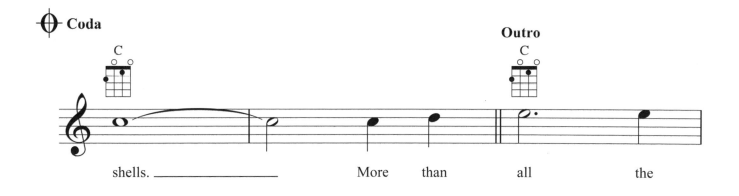

D.S. al Coda

for each star that twin - kles in the blue. Pearl - y

Coda

Outro

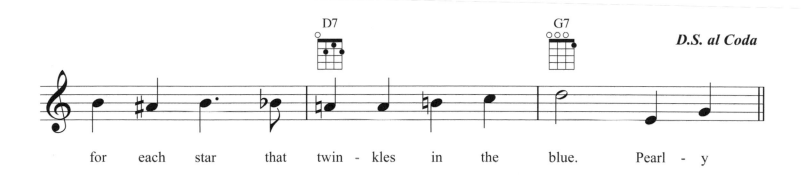

shells. _____ More than all the

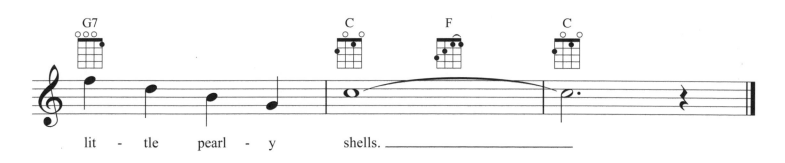

lit - tle pearl - y shells. _____

Puff the Magic Dragon

Words and Music by Lenny Lipton and Peter Yarrow

First note

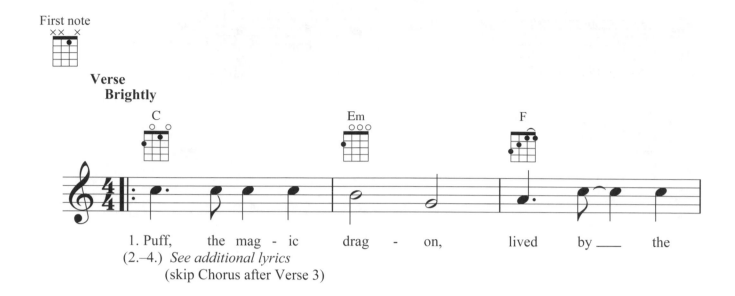

Verse
Brightly

1. Puff, the mag - ic drag - on, lived by ___ the
(2.–4.) *See additional lyrics*
(skip Chorus after Verse 3)

sea and frol - icked in ___ the au - tumn mist ___ in a

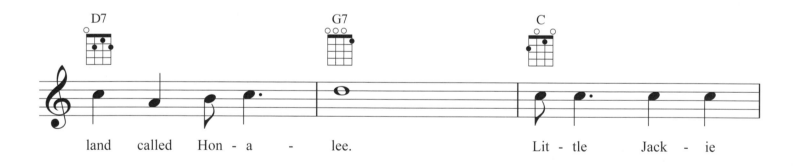

land called Hon - a - lee. Lit - tle Jack - ie

Pa - per loved that ras - cal Puff, and

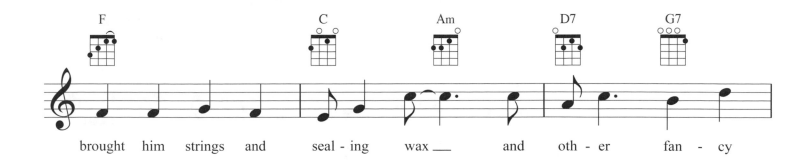

brought him strings and seal-ing wax ___ and oth-er fan - cy

Chorus

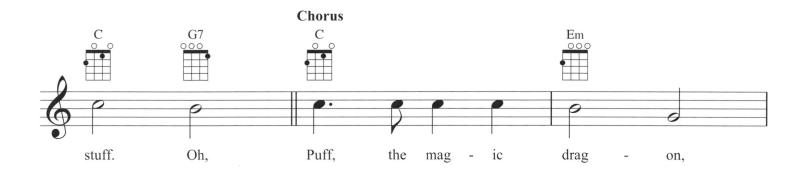

stuff. Oh, Puff, the mag - ic drag - on,

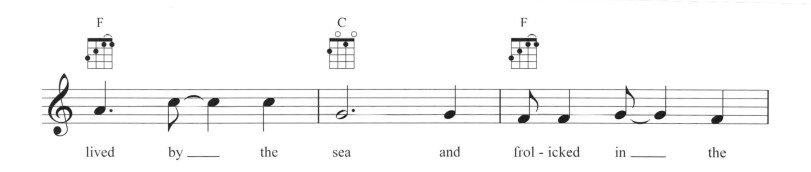

lived by ___ the sea and frol - icked in ___ the

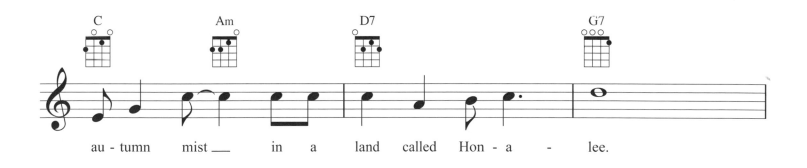

au - tumn mist ___ in a land called Hon - a - lee.

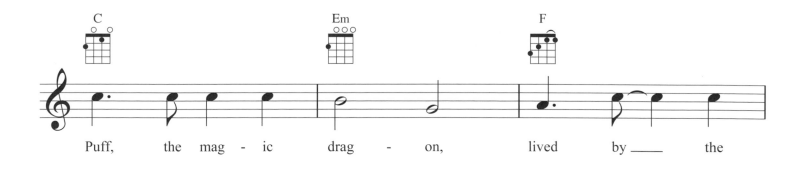

Puff, the mag - ic drag - on, lived by ___ the

sea   and   frol-icked   in ____   the   au - tumn   mist ___   in a

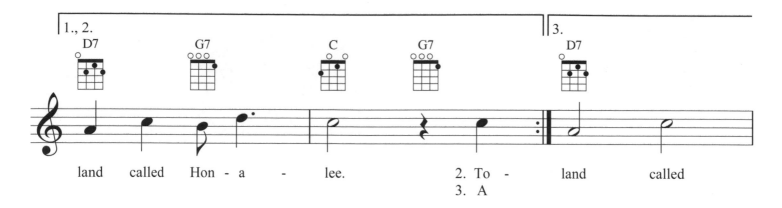

land   called   Hon - a - lee.   2. To - land   called
                                          3. A

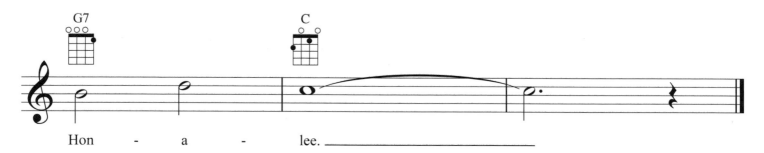

Hon - a - lee. _____

Additional Lyrics

2. Together they would travel on a boat with billowed sail,
And Jackie kept a lookout perched on Puff's gigantic tail.
Noble kings and princes would bow whenever they came.
Pirate ships would lower their flags when Puff roared out his name.

3. A dragon lives forever, but not so little boys.
Painted wings and giants' rings make way for other toys.
One gray night it happened; Jackie Paper came no more,
And Puff, that mighty dragon, he ceased his fearless roar. *(To Verse 4)*

4. His head was bent in sorrow, green scales fell like rain.
Puff no longer went to play along the Cherry Lane.
Without his lifelong friend, Puff could not be brave.
So Puff, that mighty dragon, sadly slipped into his cave.

The Rainbow Connection

from THE MUPPET MOVIE

Words and Music by Paul Williams and Kenneth L. Ascher

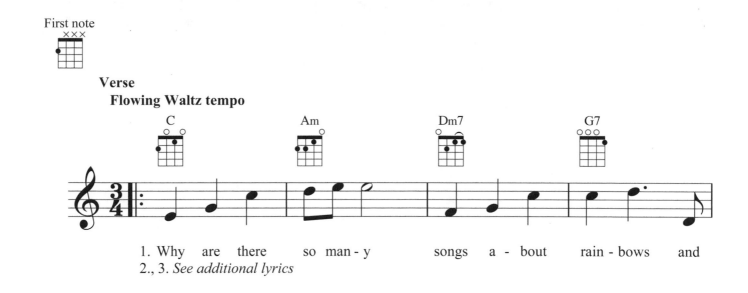

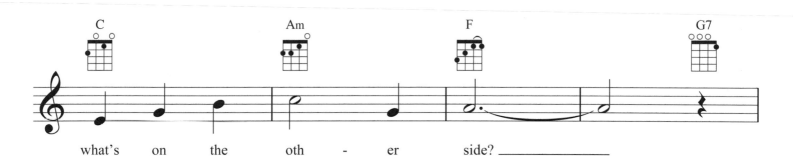

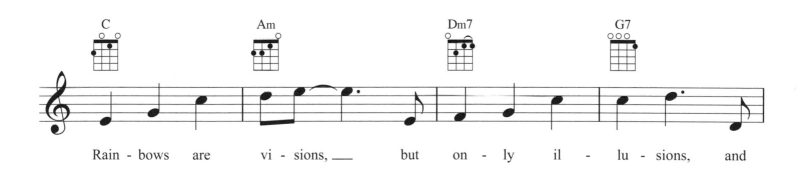

Pre-Chorus

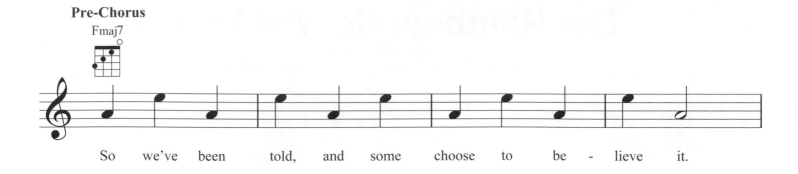

So we've been told, and some choose to be - lieve it.

I know they're wrong; wait and see. _____

Chorus

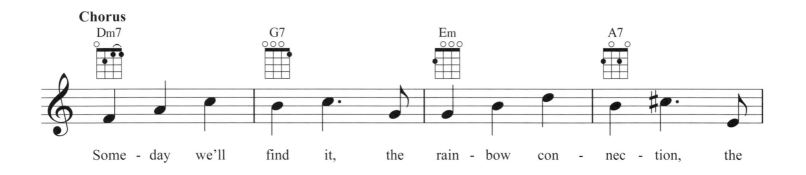

Some - day we'll find it, the rain - bow con - nec - tion, the

To Coda

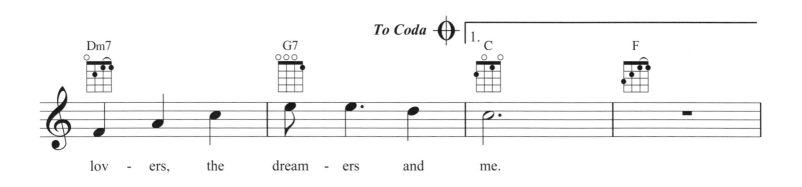

lov - ers, the dream - ers and me.

Bridge

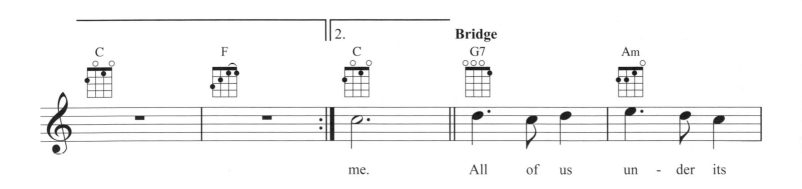

me. All of us un - der its

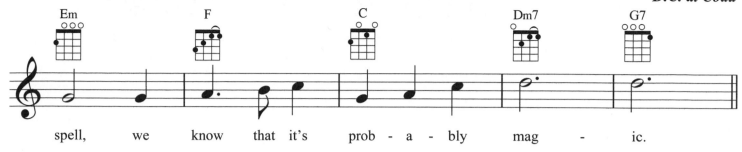

spell,   we   know   that it's   prob - a - bly   mag -   ic.

Coda

Outro

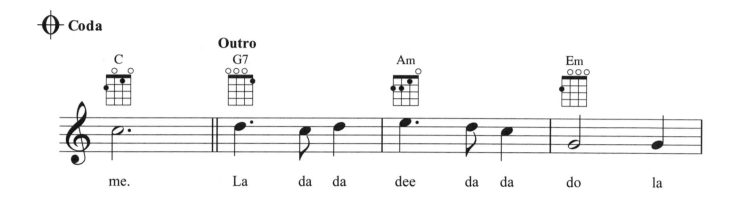

me.   La   da da   dee   da da   do   la

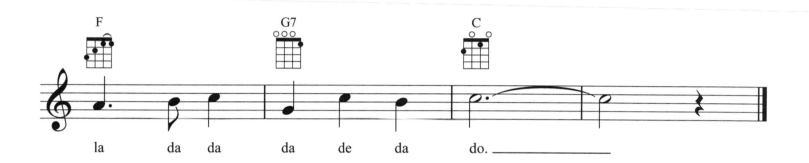

la   da da   da de da   do. _____

Additional Lyrics

2. Who said that ev'ry wish would be heard and answered
   When wished on the morning star?
   Somebody thought of that and someone believed it;
   Look what it's done so far.
   What's so amazing that keeps us stargazing,
   And what do we think we might see?

3. Have you been half asleep and have you heard voices?
   I've heard them calling my name.
   Is this the sweet sound that calls the young sailors?
   The voice might be one and the same.
   I've heard it too many times to ignore it;
   It's something that I'm s'posed to be.

Put a Little Love in Your Heart

Words and Music by Jimmy Holiday, Randy Myers and Jackie DeShannon

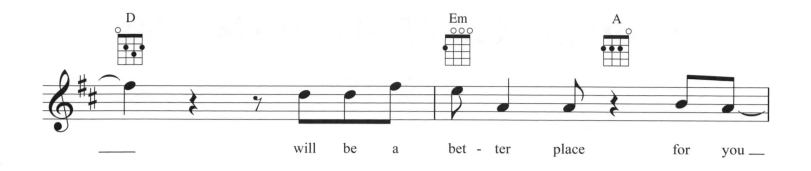

will be a bet - ter place for you

and me. You just wait

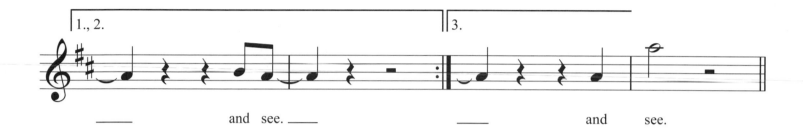

1., 2. | and see. | 3. | and see.

Outro

Repeat and fade

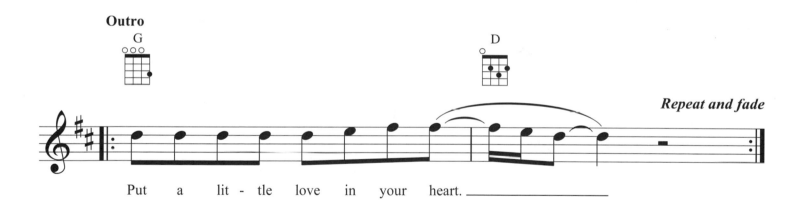

Put a lit - tle love in your heart.

Additional Lyrics

2. Another day goes by, and still the children cry.
   Put a little love in your heart.
   If you want the world to know we won't let hatred grow,
   Put a little love in your heart.

3. Take a good look around, and if you're lookin' down,
   Put a little love in your heart.
   I hope when you decide, kindness will be your guide.
   Put a little love in your heart.

Raindrops Keep Fallin' on My Head

Lyric by Hal David
Music by Burt Bacharach

Rhythm of Love

Words and Music by Tim Lopez

morn - ing sun, you're ___ mine, ___ all _____

mine. Play the mu - sic ___ low ___ and sway ___ to the rhy - thm of ___

Bridge

___ love.   When the moon is

low, _____   we can dance in

slow _____ mo - tion and all your ___

tears   will ___ sub - side. All your tears _____ will ___

Additional Lyrics

2. Well, my heart beats like a drum,
   A guitar string to the strum,
   A beautiful song to be sung.
   She's got blue eyes, deep like the sea,
   That roll back when she's laughing at me.
   She rises up like the tide the moment her lips meet mine.

D.S. And long after I've gone, you'll still be humming along.
     And I will keep you in my mind, the way you make love so fine.

Stand by Your Man

Words and Music by Tammy Wynette and Billy Sherrill

Riptide

Words and Music by Vance Joy

1. I was scared of den - tists and the dark. ___
2. There's this mov - ie that ___ I think you'll like. ___ This

I was scared of pret - ty girls ___ and start - ing con - ver - sa - tions. ___ All ___
guy de - cides to quit his job ___ and heads to New York Cit - y. ___ This

___ my ___ friends ___ are turn - ing green; ___ you're the
cow - boy's ___ run - ning from him - self, ___ and

ma - gi - cian's ___ as - sist - ant in their dream. ___ }
she's been liv - ing on ___ the high - est shelf. ___ }

Ah

Pre-Chorus

ooh. ___ Ah oh, ___ and they

Chorus

come _ un - stuck. _____ La - dy, ___ run-ning down _ to the

rip - tide, tak - en a - way __ to the dark side, I wan-na be ___ your

left - hand _ man. ___ I love you when you're sing - ing that

song, _ and I got a lump _ in my throat 'cause you're gon - na sing __ the words __

1.
_____ wrong.

2.
_____ wrong.

(Instrumental)

Bridge

I just wan - na, I just wan - na know ___

if you're gon - na, if you're gon - na stay. ___

I just got - ta, I just got - ta know; ___

I can't have ___ it, I can't have ___ it an - y oth - er way. I

swear she's des - tined for the screen;

clos - est thing to Mi - chelle Pfeif - fer that you've ev - er seen. Oh, ___

Sing

from SESAME STREET
Words and Music by Joe Raposo

Sing! _____ Sing a song, _____ _____ make it sim - ple to last your whole life long. _____ Don't wor - ry that it's not good e - nough for an - y - one else to hear. Sing! _____ Sing a song. _____

Outro

Repeat and fade

La la do la da, la da la do la da, la da da la do la da. ____

Singin' in the Rain

Lyric by Arthur Freed
Music by Nacio Herb Brown

read - y for love. Let the storm - y clouds

chase ev - 'ry - one _____ from the place. Come

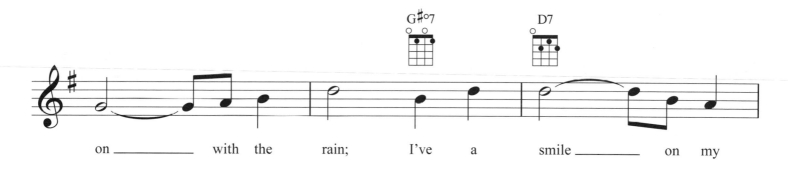

on _____ with the rain; I've a smile _____ on my

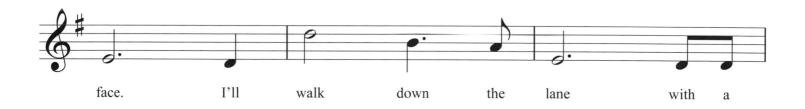

face. I'll walk down the lane with a

hap - py re - frain, and sing - in', _____ just

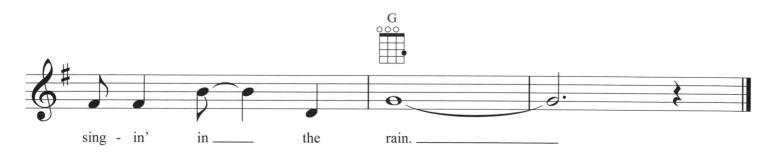

sing - in' in ____ the rain. _____

Sweet Caroline

Words and Music by Neil Diamond

Interlude

Outro-Chorus

Sweet Car - o - line, _____ good times

nev - er seemed _ so good.

Sweet Car - o - line, _____ I be - lieve _

Repeat and fade

_____ they nev - er could. _____

Take Me Home, Country Roads

Words and Music by John Denver, Bill Danoff and Taffy Nivert

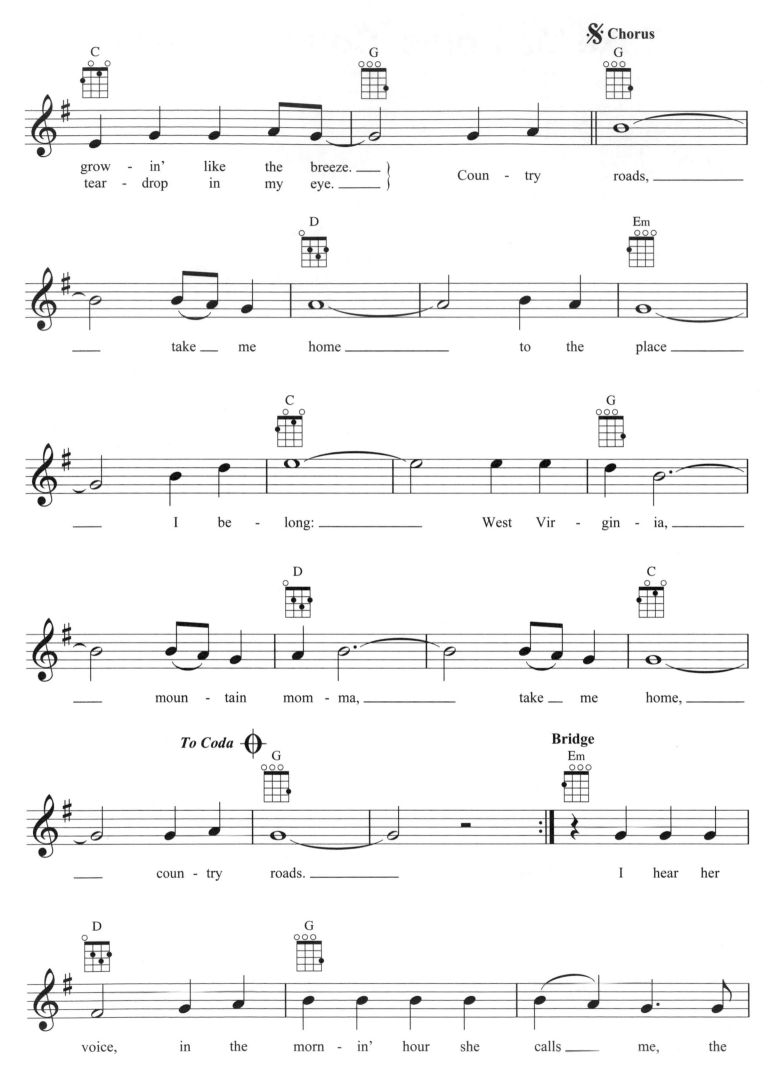

That's Amoré
(That's Love)

from the Paramount Picture THE CADDY
Words by Jack Brooks
Music by Harry Warren

First note

Chorus
Moderately

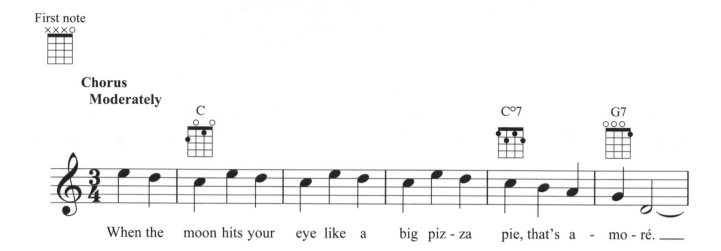

When the moon hits your eye like a big piz - za pie, that's a - mo - ré. ___

___ When the world seems to shine like you've had too much

wine, that's a - mo - ré. ___ Bells will ring, ting - a - ling - a -

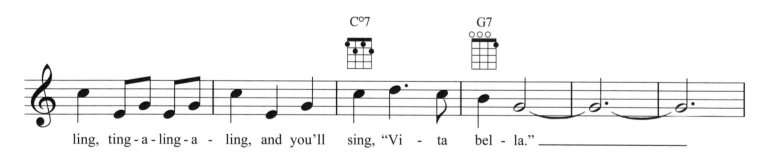

ling, ting - a - ling - a - ling, and you'll sing, "Vi - ta bel - la." ___

Hearts will play, tip-py-tip-py - tay, tip-py-tip-py - tay like a gay tar - an -

This Land Is Your Land

Words and Music by Woody Guthrie

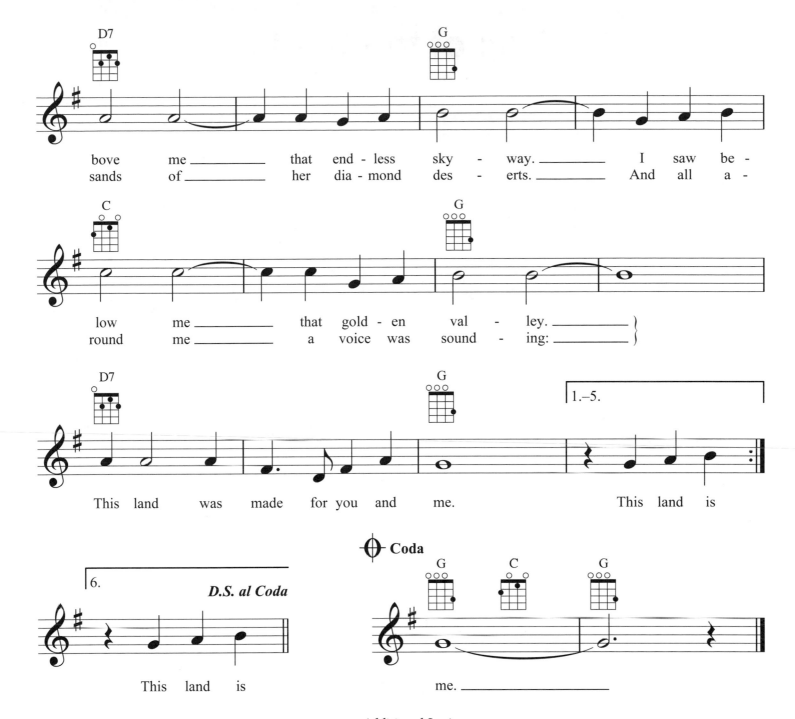

Additional Lyrics

3. When the sun came shining, and I was strolling,
   And the wheat fields waving, and the dust clouds rolling,
   As the fog was lifting, a voice was chanting:
   This land was made for you and me.

4. As I went walking, I saw a sign there,
   And on the sign it said, "No Trespassing,"
   But on the other side it didn't say nothing;
   That side was made for you and me.

5. In the shadow of the steeple, I saw my people.
   By the relief office, I saw my people.
   As they stood there hungry, I stood there asking:
   Is this land made for you and me?

6. Nobody living can ever stop me
   As I go walking that freedom highway.
   Nobody living can ever make me turn back;
   This land was made for you and me.

Top of the World

Words and Music by John Bettis and Richard Carpenter

First note

Verse
Moderately, in 2

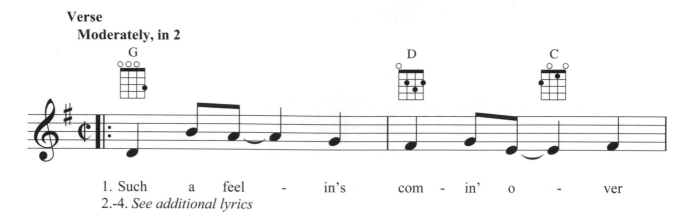

1. Such a feel - in's com - in' o - ver
2.-4. *See additional lyrics*

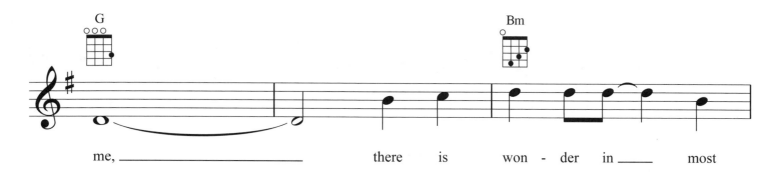

me, _____ there is won - der in ___ most

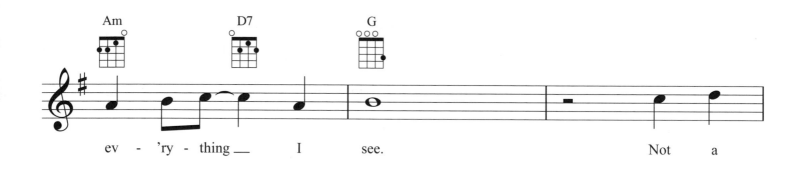

ev - 'ry - thing ___ I see. Not a

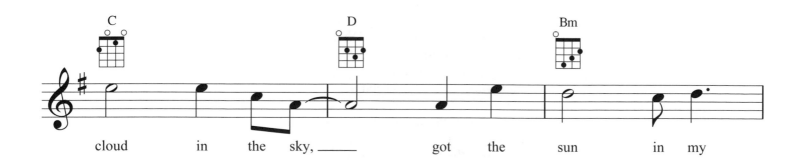

cloud in the sky, ___ got the sun in my

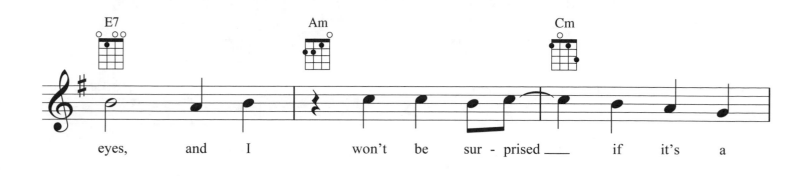

eyes,   and   I   won't   be   sur - prised ___   if   it's   a

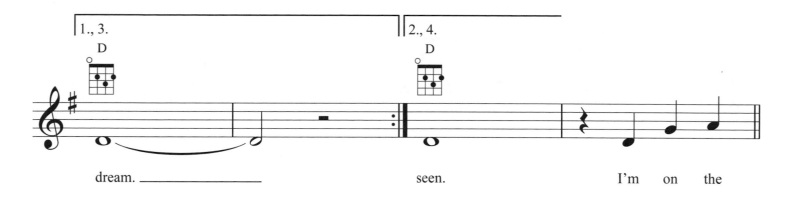

1., 3.   **2., 4.**

dream. _____   seen.   I'm   on   the

Chorus

top   of   the   world _____ look - in'   down   on   cre - a -

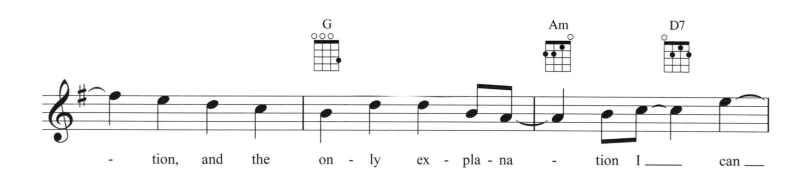

- tion,   and   the   on - ly   ex - pla - na -   tion   I ___   can ___

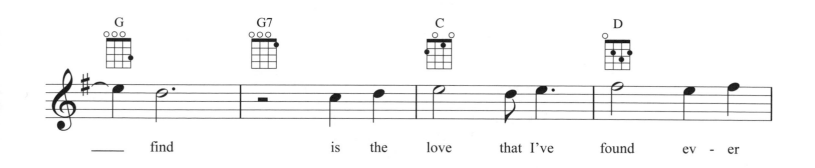

___ find   is   the   love   that   I've   found   ev - er

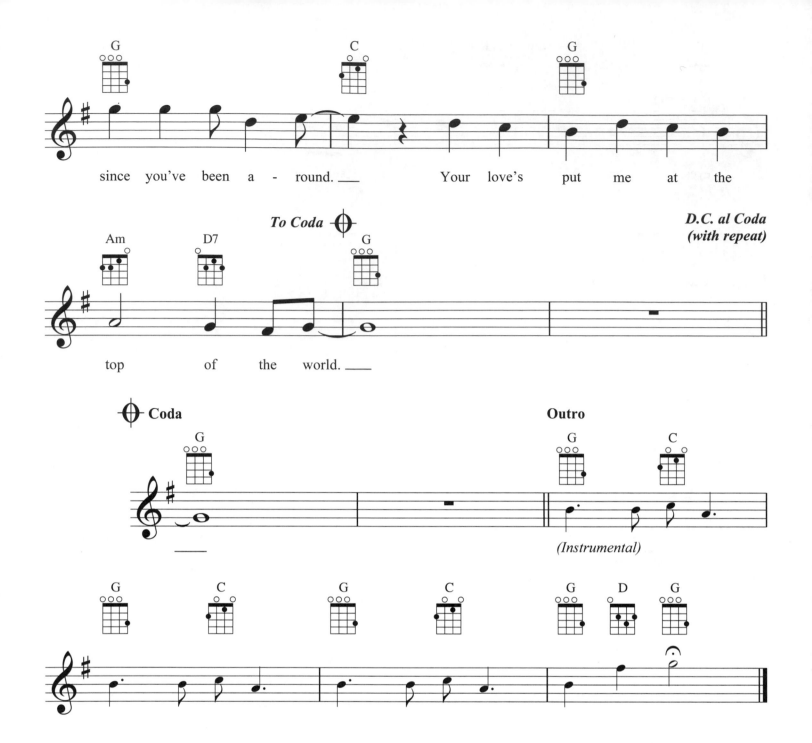

Additional Lyrics

2. Everything I want the world to be
   Is now coming true especially for me.
   And the reason is clear; it's because you are here.
   You're the nearest thing to heaven that I've seen.

3. Something in the wind has learned my name,
   And it's telling me that things are not the same.
   In the leaves on the trees and the touch of the breeze,
   There's a pleasing sense of happiness for me.

4. There is only one wish on my mind:
   When this day is through, I hope that I will find
   That tomorrow will be just the same for you and me.
   All I need will be mine if you are here.

We Are the World

Words and Music by Lionel Richie and Michael Jackson

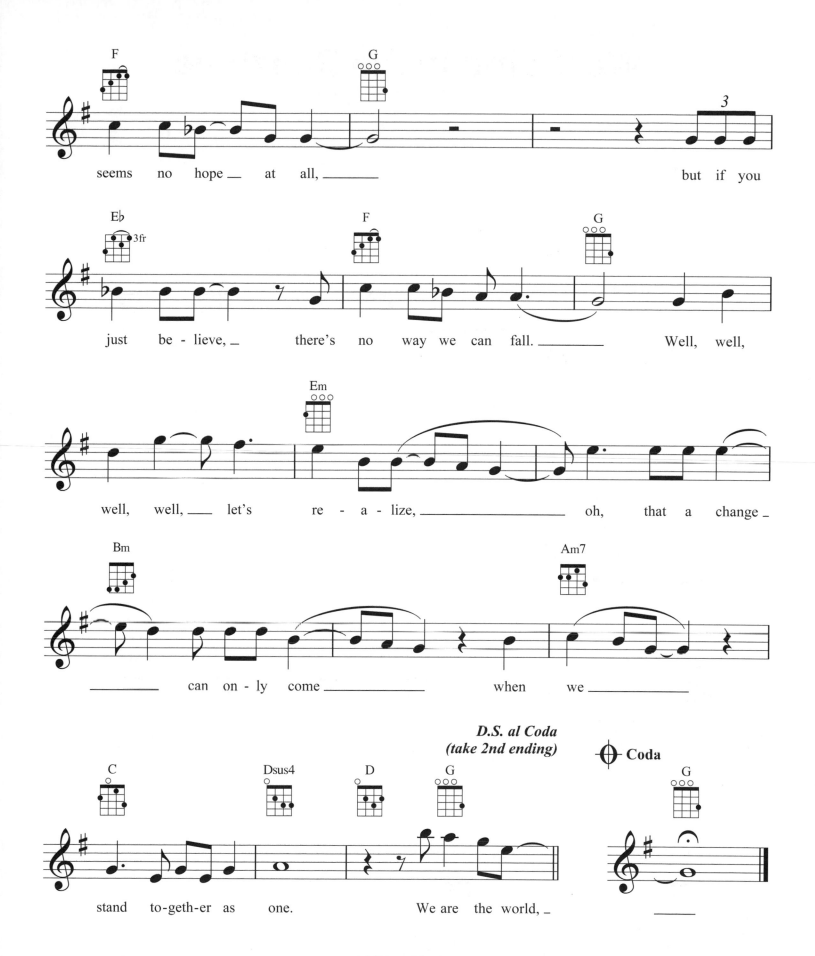

seems no hope — at all, _____ but if you

just be - lieve, _ there's no way we can fall. _____ Well, well,

well, well, ___ let's re - a - lize, _____ oh, that a change _

_____ can on - ly come _____ when we _____

D.S. al Coda
(take 2nd ending) ⊕ **Coda**

stand to-geth-er as one. We are the world, _ _____

Additional Lyrics

2. We can't go on pretending day by day
That someone, somewhere will soon make a change.
We are all a part of God's great big family,
And the truth, you know: love is all we need.

3. Send them your heart so they know that someone cares,
And their lives will be stronger and free.
As God has shown us by turning stone to bread,
And so we all must lend a helping hand.

We'll Sing in the Sunshine

Words and Music by Gale Garnett

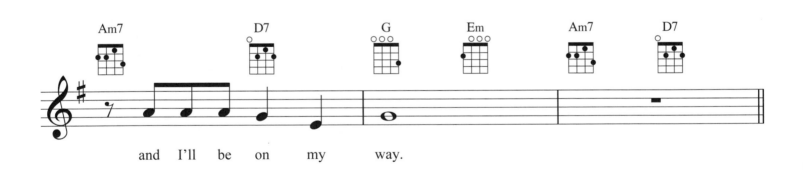

1. I   will   nev - er   love ____ you; ____   the   cost   of   love's   too   dear. ____
2. sing   to   you   each morn - ing, ____   I'll   kiss   you   ev - 'ry   night. ____
3. dad - dy,   he   once told ____ me: ____   don't   love   you   an - y   man, ____
4. when   our   year   has   end - ed ____   and   I   have   gone   a - way, ____

What a Wonderful World

Words and Music by George David Weiss and Bob Thiele

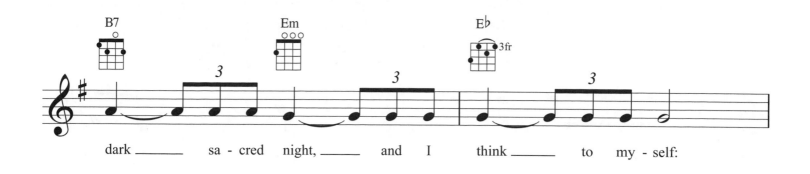

dark _____ sa - cred night, _____ and I think _____ to my - self:

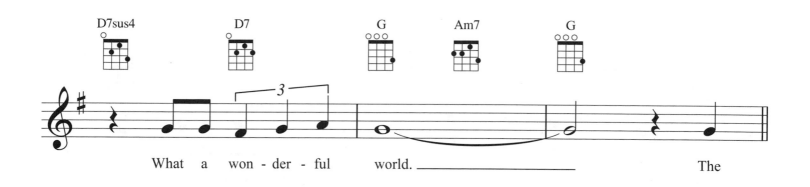

What a won - der - ful world. _____ The

Bridge

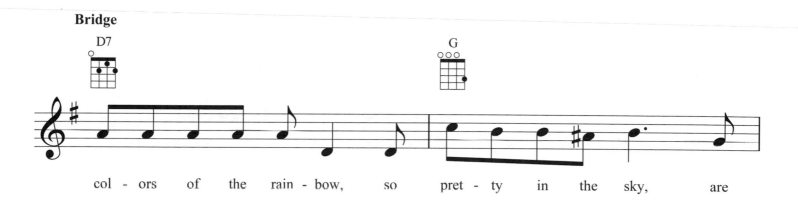

col - ors of the rain - bow, so pret - ty in the sky, are

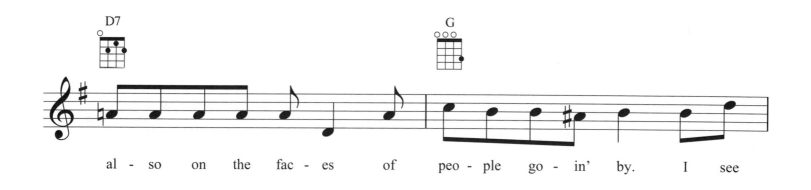

al - so on the fac - es of peo - ple go - in' by. I see

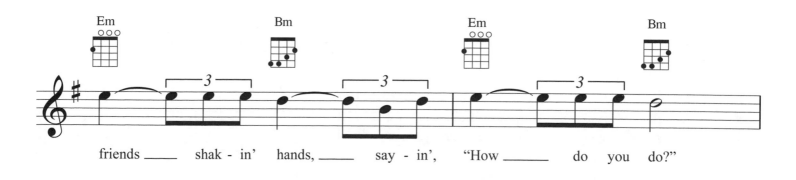

friends _____ shak - in' hands, _____ say - in', "How _____ do you do?"

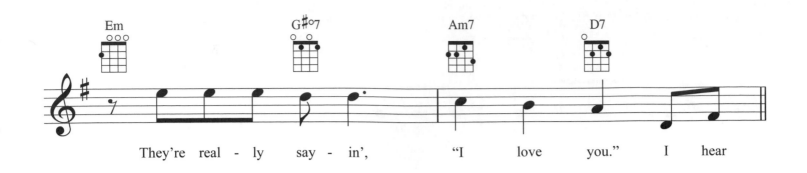

They're real - ly say - in', "I love you." I hear

Outro-Verse

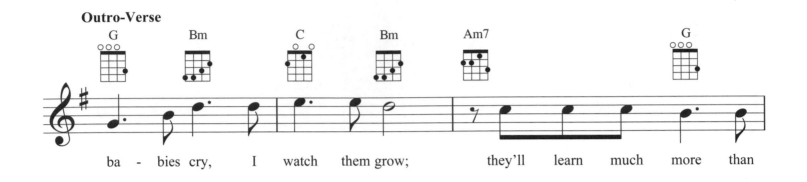

ba - bies cry, I watch them grow; they'll learn much more than

I'll _____ ev - er know, _____ and I think _____ to my - self:

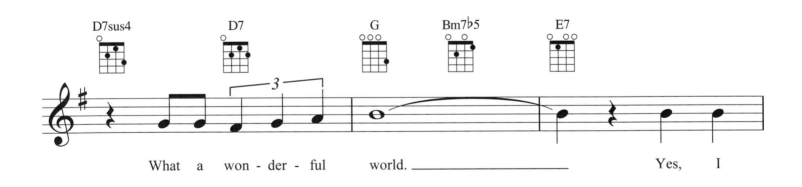

What a won - der - ful world. _____ Yes, I

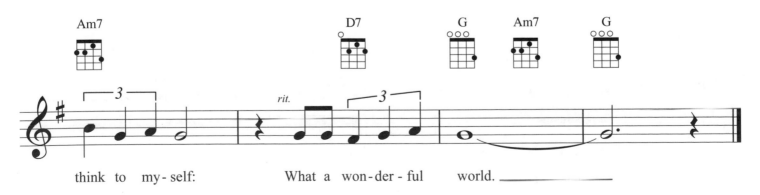

think to my - self: What a won - der - ful world. _____

When I'm Sixty-Four

Words and Music by John Lennon and Paul McCartney

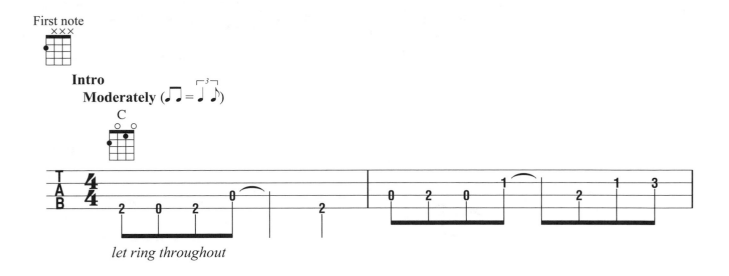

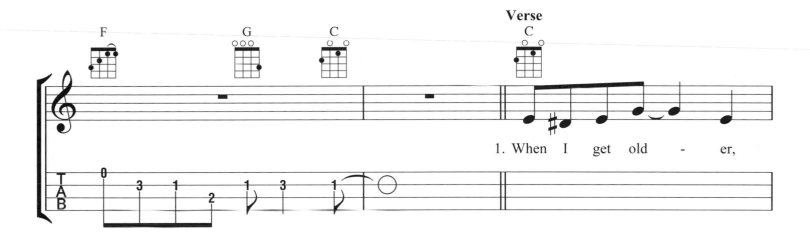

bot - tle of wine? __   If I'd been out __ till   quar - ter to three, __

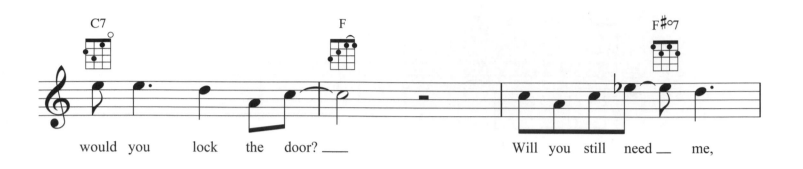

would you lock the door? ___   Will you still need __ me,

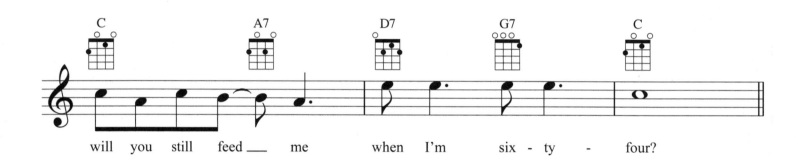

will you still feed ___ me   when I'm six - ty - four?

Bridge

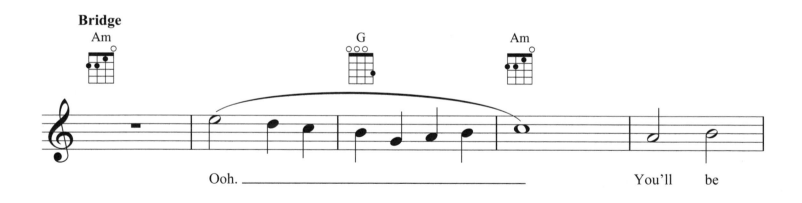

Ooh. _____   You'll be

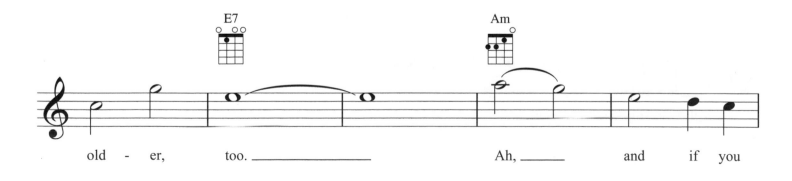

old - er, too. _____   Ah, _____ and if you

Dm   F   G

say the word, _____   I   could stay   with

C   G

you.

%· **Verse**

C

2. I could be hand - y mend - ing a fuse ___   when your lights have gone. __
3. Send me a post - card, drop me a line ___   stat - ing point of view. __

G7

___   You can knit a sweat-er by the fire - side; __
___   In - di - cate pre - cise - ly what you mean to say, __

N.C.   C

Sun - day morn - ing,   go for a ride. __   Do - ing the gar - den,
yours sin - cere - ly wast - ing a - way. __   Give me your an - swer,

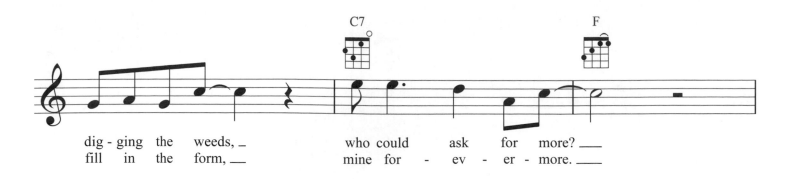

dig - ging the weeds, ___ who could ask for more? ___
fill in the form, ___ mine for - ev - er - more. ___

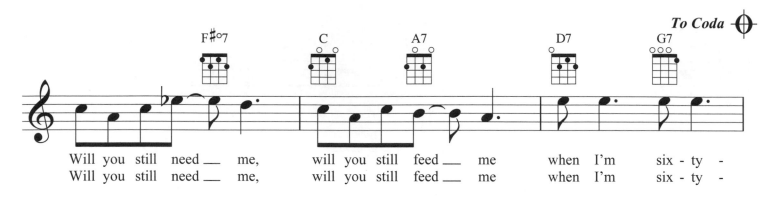

To Coda ⊕

Will you still need ___ me, will you still feed ___ me when I'm six - ty -
Will you still need ___ me, will you still feed ___ me when I'm six - ty -

Bridge

four? Ev - 'ry sum - mer we can rent a cot - tage in the Isle of Wight ___

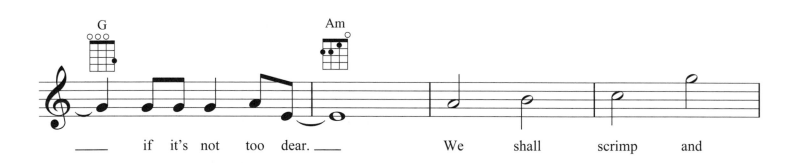

___ if it's not too dear. ___ We shall scrimp and

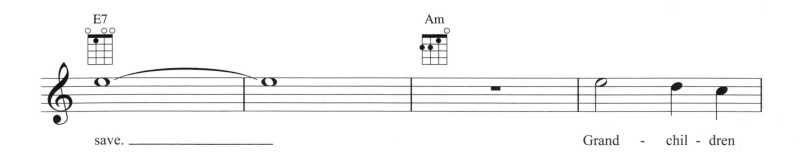

save. _____ Grand - chil - dren

132

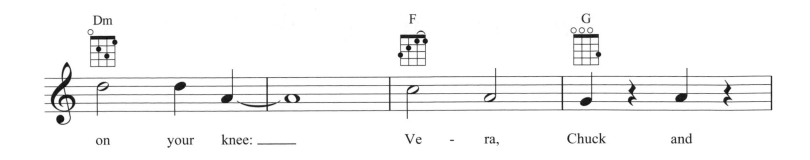

on   your   knee: _____   Ve -   ra,   Chuck   and

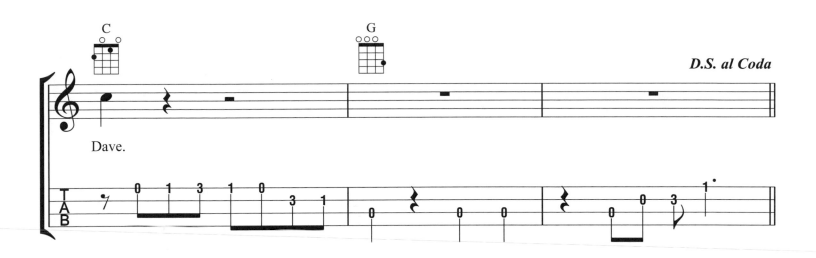

D.S. al Coda

Dave.

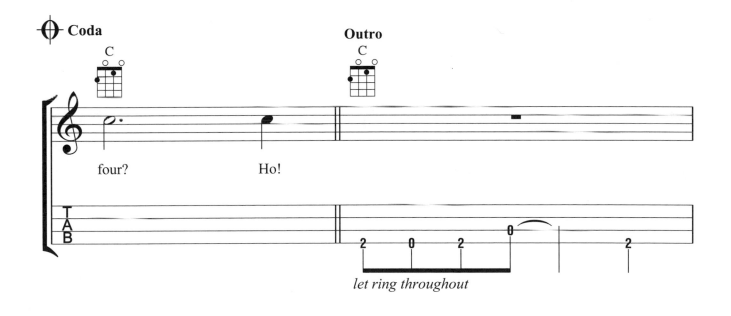

Coda

four?   Ho!

Outro

let ring throughout

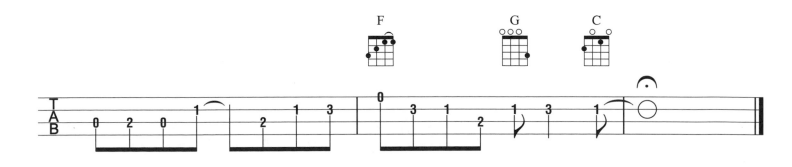

You Are My Sunshine

Words and Music by Jimmie Davis

Additional Lyrics

2. I'll always love you and make you happy
   If you will only say the same.
   But if you leave me to love another,
   You'll regret it all someday.

3. You told me once, dear, you really loved me
   And no one else could come between.
   But now you've left me and love another;
   You have shattered all my dreams.

MORE BOOKS FOR BARITONE UKULELE PLAYERS

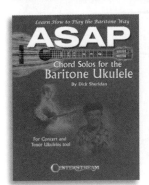

ASAP CHORD SOLOS FOR THE BARITONE UKULELE
LEARN HOW TO PLAY THE BARITONE WAY
by Dick Sheridan
Centerstream Publications

Enjoy this super mix of jazz, blues, barbershop, gospel, classical, ethnic, folk and old favorites! This collection features 27 solos arranged with just chord diagrams for players at all levels of ability. Songs include: Aura Lee • Down by the Old Mill Stream • Hard Times Come Again No More • My Wild Irish Rose • Twelve-Bar Blues • Liebestraum • Ja-Da • My Buddy • Sweet Adeline • In the Bleak Midwinter • Memories • Toyland • Dark Eyes • and more. Each solo is preceded by a page of background information with interesting comments about the composers and the songs themselves. Introductory text provides instructions, detailed guidelines, helpful playing tips, and useful insights.

00145630 Book $19.99

JUMPIN' JIM'S THE BARI BEST
compiled & arranged by Jim Beloff
Flea Market Music, Inc.

At last! Here is a handy songbook arranged especially for baritone ukulele (DGBE) tuning. 30 great songs, including: Heart and Soul • The Christmas Song • Five Foot Two, Eyes of Blue • Georgia on My Mind • When I'm Sixty-Four • I'll See You in My Dreams • Makin' Love Ukulele Style • Moon River • Blue Skies • and many more. Also includes a complete chord chart, vintage baritone uke advertising, and the history of the Favilla baritone uke by Tom Favilla.

00695926 Book $19.95

HAL LEONARD BARITONE UKULELE CHORD FINDER

Learn to play chords on the baritone uke with this comprehensive, yet easy-to-use book. Contains more than 1,000 chord diagrams for the 28 most important chord types, including three voicings for each chord. Also includes a lesson on chord construction and a fingerboard chart of the baritone ukulele neck!

00696377 Book.....................................$6.99

THE DAILY UKULELE – BARITONE EDITION
compiled and arranged by Liz and Jim Beloff

Now baritone ukulele players can have fun every day, too! Strum a different song every day with easy arrangements of 365 of your favorite songs in one big songbook! *The Daily Ukulele* features ukulele arrangements with melody, lyrics and uke chord grids in ukulele-friendly keys that are particularly suited for groups of one to one hundred to play and sing. Includes favorites by the Beatles, Beach Boys and Bob Dylan, folk songs, pop songs, kids' songs, Christmas carols and Broadway and Hollywood tunes, all with a spiral binding for ease of use. Also features a Tips & Techniques section, chord chart, and vintage ukulele-themed photos and art throughout. *The Daily Ukulele* offers ukulele fun all year long!

00121280 Book $39.99

FIDDLE TUNES FOR BARITONE UKULELE
by Dick Sheridan
Centerstream Publications

The lively, dynamic melodies associated with the fiddle can now be shared with the ukulele without losing any of the excitement, beauty and drive. This collection features 55 fun-filled favorites in standard notation and tablature with chord symbols and diagrams, plus online access to audio recordings of examples of the music. Songs include: Arkansas Traveler • Bully of the Town • Cherish the Ladies • Flop-Eared Mule • Harvest Home • Irish Washerwoman • Miss McLeod's Reel • Ragtime Annie • Sailor's Hornpipe • Turkey in the Straw • and more.

00153260 Book/Online Audio.......................................$19.99

HAL LEONARD BARITONE UKULELE METHOD – BOOK 1
by Lil' Rev

This comprehensive, easy-to-use beginner's guide by uke master Lil' Rev is designed for anyone just learning to play baritone ukulele. It teaches: tuning; music reading and tablature; melody playing; chords & scales; strumming; tremolo; the history of the instrument; and much more! Students will learn lots of fun songs in various styles.

00696552 Book Only $6.99
00696564 Book/Online Audio.......................................$10.99